Using Punches

by Julie Hickey

I can't remember when my love affair with punches began. I was always an avid stamper, and I used to think that punches were only for making animal shapes such as rabbits. Then I was introduced to the daisy punch, and I was totally hooked!

I love the simplicity of punched cards: the variety of effects that you can create by using different papers and cards, and the fact that you can mix them with wire, beads and threads to give added interest.

There is so much that you can do with just a square punch: you can use the squares to mount on to or create a simple square or a rectangular aperture. You can then use another punch to punch the square waste from a card, creating a square with a shaped hole in it.

There are so many different punches available now, and I feel sure that whether you are a punch addict or just embarking on your journey of discovery, you will find many hints and tips in this section to help you get more from your punches.

Enjoy the project on the following pages, use it to get your creativity flowing and create your own fabulous punched greetings cards.

Julie x

Encyclopedia
of Cardmaking
Techniques

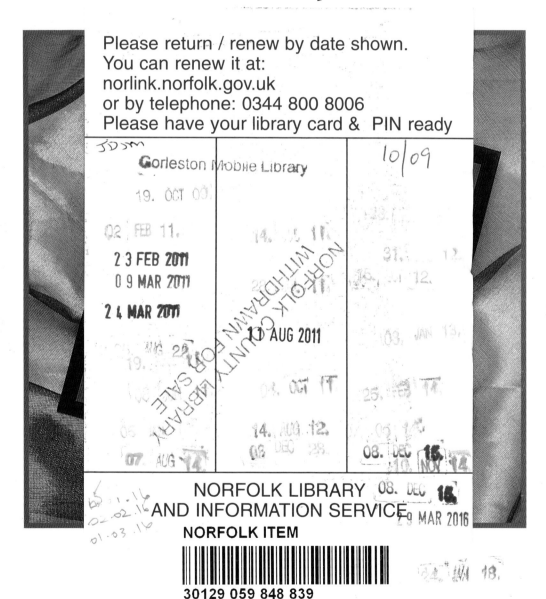
SEARCH PRESS

First published in Great Britain 2007

Search Press Limited
Wellwood, North Farm Road,
Tunbridge Wells, Kent TN2 3DR

Reprinted 2008 (twice)

Based on the following books from the *Handmade Greetings Cards* series published by Search Press:

Punched Greetings Cards by Julie Hickey (2003)
Embossed Greetings Cards by Carol Wallis (2004)
Eyelet Greetings Cards by Polly Pinder (2005)
Glitter Greetings Cards by Polly Pinder (2005)
Metal & Wire Greetings Cards by Julie Hickey (2002)
Polymer Clay Greetings Cards by Candida Woolhouse (2002)
Silk Ribbon Greetings Cards by Ann Cox (2005)
Card & Thread Greetings Cards by Polly Pinder (2004)
Quick Parchment Greetings Cards by Janet Wilson (2005)
Glass Painted Greetings Cards by Judy Balchin (2002)
Tea Bag Folded Greetings Cards by Kim Reigate (2003)
Peel-Off Greetings Cards by Judy Balchin (2002)
Rubber Stamped Greetings Cards by
Melanie Hendrick (2002)
Watercolour Greetings Cards by Jane Greenwood (2004)
Beaded Greetings Cards by Patricia Wing (2005)
Quilled Greetings Cards by Diane Crane (2005)
Three-Dimensional Greetings Cards by Dawn Allen (2005)
Iris Folded Greetings Cards by Michelle Powell (2004)

Text copyright © Julie Hickey, Carol Wallis, Polly Pinder,
Candida Woolhouse, Ann Cox, Janet Wilson, Judy Balchin,
Kim Reigate, Melanie Hendrick, Jane Greenwood,
Patricia Wing, Diane Crane, Dawn Allen and Michelle Powell

Photographs by Charlotte de la Bédoyère, Search Press
Studios and Roddy Paine Photographic Studios

Photographs and design copyright © Search Press Ltd. 2007

ISBN: 978-1-84448-283-2
74S-S941

Contents

Techniques

Punches are very versatile: you do not have to use them just for the shape that they punch. A square punch can create square or rectangular apertures in cards, or punched squares or diamonds for layering other shapes on to. You can punch out different shapes and use the square punch upside down around the hole to create a square with a shaped hole in it.

Tip
When using the punch upside down, push down gently until you feel the punch bite, position your paper or card, then push all the way down to punch out the shape.

Making a square aperture

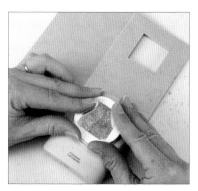

1. Work with the card open. Put the punch in from the top, as far as it will go. Judge by eye that the punch is in the middle of the card, or use a set square to measure it.

2. Make a second aperture at the bottom of the card, in the same way.

3. You can not punch out a third square in the middle, as the punch will not reach that far. Punch out a square in a different colour and place it in the middle of the card as shown. Stick it in place with double-sided tape.

Making a rectangular aperture

1. Work with the card open. Put the square punch in from the side and line up the top of the card with the edge of the punch. Push the punch in as far as it will go and punch.

2. Line the punch up in the same way at the bottom of the card and punch out another square.

3. Punch two overlapping squares in the middle of the card to finish the long aperture.

Making a three aperture card

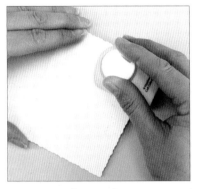

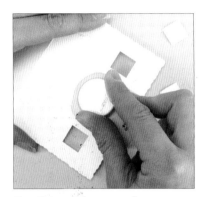

1. Open the card. Line up the small square punch with the top of the card and punch out a square.

2. Do the same at the bottom of the card.

3. Centre the punch between the two apertures by eye and punch out the middle square.

Making an opening card with a punch

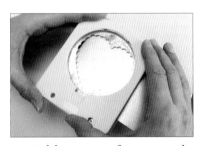

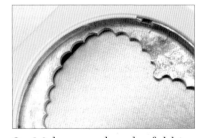

1. Fold a piece of paper and place it in the upside-down punch, so that you can see clearly where the punch will cut the shape.

2. Make sure that the fold in the paper is inside the punch area. Here the fold can just be seen on the left-hand side of the heart shape.

3. When the shape is punched, the fold will remain intact, and the shape will open out to make a gift tag or small card.

Using the waste

1. Punch out a daisy and keep the waste paper out of which it has been punched. The punched out daisy itself can be used for another card.

2. Hold a square punch upside down and feed in the waste paper. I have marked the centre points on the metal underside of my punch. Line the daisy petals up with the marks.

3. Punch out the square. The daisy-shaped hole will be centred in the middle of the square.

Border punches

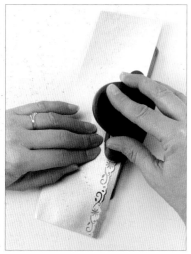

1. Place the paper in the border punch. Make sure it is pushed in and lines up with the back plate, and punch. Move the punched strip along and line it up with the pattern on the base of the punch. Punch again, line up again and punch until the whole strip is punched out.

2. When you have completed your border, pull off the waste paper edge.

3. You can cut strips of paper in different widths and use the border punch on both sides, as shown. I have found that a 3cm (1¼in) strip works well, but by altering the width you can achieve different looks.

The finished panel

Sponging through a stencil

1. Punch a flower shape out of card to make a stencil. Many punches are great for creating stencils. Have fun discovering which shapes work best.

2. Position the stencil on your card, and using a piece of cosmetic sponge and an inkpad, sponge through the stencil.

Here are some of the beautiful effects you can achieve using punches with the techniques shown.

Daisies with Wire

The first project had to feature the daisy punch! I have combined it with my second favourite punch: the square. I have used a special corner cutter on the squares, then wrapped them with thread. The stems of the daisies are made by bending and shaping wire to finish the look.

The template for the daisy stems

You will need

Daisy, square and corner cutter punches

Blackcurrant card blank, 10 x 21cm (3⅞ x 8¼in)

Blackcurrant and silver card

22g silver wire, round-nosed pliers and wire cutters

Double-sided tape

All-purpose glue and paper pricking tool

Dimensional glue

Glue pen

Silver metallic thread

Scissors

Set square

Purple flat-backed crystals

1. Punch out three squares from silver metallic card.

2. Use a square corner cutter to cut notches in each corner of all the squares.

3. Put double-sided tape on the back of the notched squares as shown.

4. Pull back a little of the backing paper from the double-sided tape on two adjacent strips. Stick the end of some metallic thread to one of the strips, as straight as possible. Take the thread to the first notch.

5. Bring the thread round to the front of the square, wrap it round one of the notched corners, then take it down at right angles, wrap it around the next corner, and so on.

6. Wrap the last corner, which is also the one you started with, cut off the thread and stick the end to the double-sided tape in a straight line.

7. Punch three daisies from purple metallic card.

8. Apply glue to the back of the purple daisies using a glue pen, and stick them in the centres of the notched silver squares.

9. Peel off the backing paper from the double-sided tape on the silver squares, and stick them to the card. I use a set square that counts outwards from the centre to help me position artwork on a card blank.

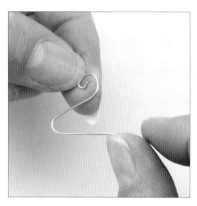

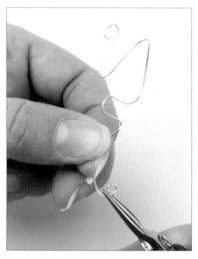

10. Cut a length of silver wire using wire cutters and use round-nosed pliers to curl the end.

11. Continue bending and shaping the wire using your fingers. Follow the template on page 10, or create your own design.

12. Make the final curl in the end of the wire using the round-nosed pliers.

13. Apply all-purpose craft glue to the back of the wire shapes using a paper pricking tool or cocktail stick, and stick the wires in place as shown. It helps to place something heavy on the wire accents while the glue dries. A big punch is ideal.

14. Place a drop of dimensional glue on to the centre of each daisy and stick a flat-backed crystal inside the wire coil.

I love this card: it is quick and easy to make, but the thread around the squares and the wire give it plenty of added interest. The sparkle from the crystals sets the daisies off beautifully.

You can create great-looking cards by using pre-embossed card blanks and adding a daisy, crystal and wire. The squares placed at an angle make diamond shapes, which totally change the finished look. You can buy flowerpot punches, or, as in the card on the far right, draw and cut your own.

14

Embossing

by Carol Wallis

I started crafting several years ago but, after dabbling in many different crafts, I found myself looking for something new. Luckily, I was visiting my local craft store when a very brief demonstration of stencil embossing was given. Short though it was – only over a lunch break – it was enough for me to be hooked! I bought some brass stencils and an embossing tool, and began a passion that has been with me ever since.

At first I had no books, instructions or tutor so I taught myself. Though I made lots of mistakes, somehow good things always emerged from them, so it was a relatively painless process. Almost before I knew it, I was producing professional cards that were inspiring others to want to learn stencil embossing, which is also known as dry embossing.

I have not looked back since the owner of my local craft store asked me to give an in-store demonstration. From little acorns, as the saying goes, and before long I began to teach and demonstrate regularly. I have made live television appearances and written articles for magazines, and I also demonstrate regularly at craft shows. I love the challenge of thinking up different ways to use stencils, and I really enjoy meeting all the people who are curious enough to come and see what I do.

One of the best things about this craft is that anyone can do it. My youngest student so far was five, and the oldest eighty-four! Both of them produced fantastic cards in next to no time. It gives me a real thrill when other people discover how simple it is to create beautiful cards, and to see their pride in what they have achieved.

I hope you enjoy making the projects in this section as much as I did, and that they will inspire you to create lots of beautiful cards.

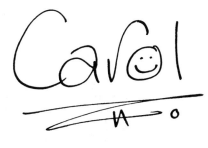

These cards for all occasions are simple, fast and fun to make using the methods shown in this section.

Hot Metal

Embossing on metal produces really dramatic effects, and is not as difficult as it looks. You do not need a light box, but you do need an unusual piece of equipment: a computer mouse mat! The reason for this is that, if you emboss metal on a flat surface, it will fold in sharp lines. If you work on the reverse of a mouse mat the yielding sponge surface results in lines that are gently curved.

For embossing on metal you will need wooden embossing tools, which are larger than metal tools. Do not try to use metal tools as they will scratch the metal foil. You will also need a wooden cocktail stick to mark out a faint line on the metal, which you then follow to emboss the lines. After embossing, the back of the raised area is filled with PVA adhesive to stop it denting.

The card is finished by mounting on several layers of card, each cut slightly smaller than the piece below. I do this by eye, so the card sizes given should be regarded as approximate.

You will need

Stencils: Dreamweaver Ginger Jar (LG626) and Celtic Heart (LL326)

Copper foil 13 x 10.5cm (5¼ x 4in)

Bronze card 21 x 13cm (8¼ x 5¼in) for mount

Green card 13 x 10.5cm (5¼ x 4in)

Gold card 13 x 10.5cm (5¼ x 4in)

Red card 13 x 10.5cm (5¼ x 4in)

Low-tack adhesive tape

Computer mouse mat

Cocktail stick

Wooden embossing tool

Wooden clothes peg

PVA adhesive

Embossing ink pad

Embossing powder: light, medium and dark metallic

Heat gun

Old scissors

Craft knife and cutting mat

Beads and a short length of wire to decorate jar

The embossing powders

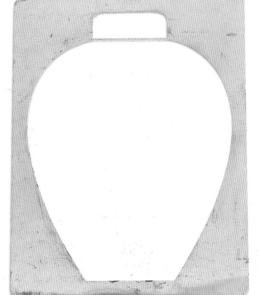

The stencils

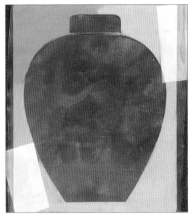

1. Working on the reverse of the mouse mat, place the jar stencil on the metal sheet. Secure with low-tack tape.

2. Using the point of a cocktail stick held at right angles to your work, trace round the outline of the jar.

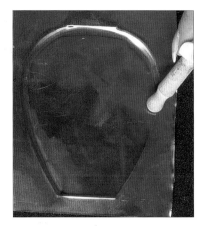

3. Turn the metal sheet over and, still working on the mouse mat, go over the outline again using the wooden tool.

4. Turn the metal sheet over. Position the heart stencil on top and fix with tape.

5. Using a cocktail stick, work carefully round the outlines of the heart design.

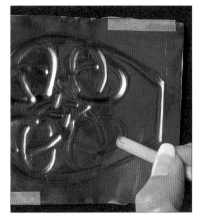

6. Turn and work on the back. Push the foil through the stencil with the blunt end of the tool.

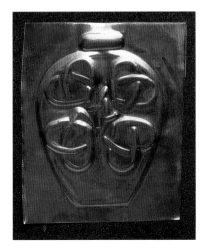

7. Turn the sheet over and remove both stencils from the front, which now has both designs raised.

8. Pat gently with the embossing ink pad to deposit small blobs of the ink randomly over the surface of the embossed design.

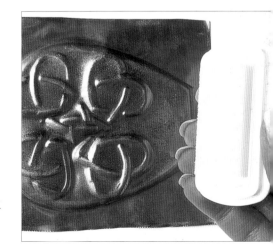

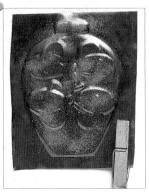

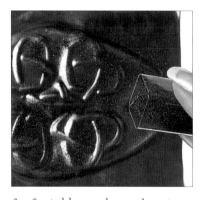

9. Sprinkle on the embossing
powder, beginning with the
darkest shade, to create an
attractive random effect.

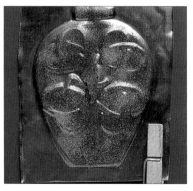

10. Sprinkle on the green
and gold powders in the same
random way, shaking off the
excess between each stage.

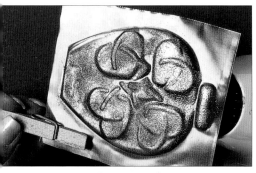

11. Hold the sheet in front
of the heat gun with the peg
'handle'. Heat the reverse until
the powders melt and go shiny.

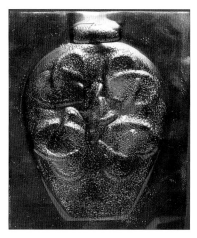

12. Leave to cool.

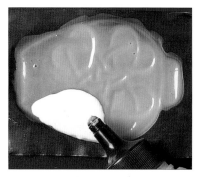

13. Turn the design over and
fill the void with PVA. The
photograph shows some of
the PVA dry and some wet.

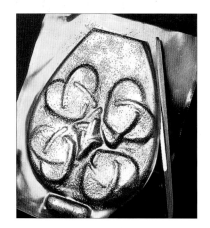

14. Leave until dry (at least
two hours), then cut out the
design using old scissors.

15. Thread beads on to the
wire and twist it to decorate
the neck of the jar. Trim the
cards for the mount, starting
with the red card, which
should measdure about 3mm
($^1/_8$in) less all round than the
bronze card. Trim about 6mm
($^1/_4$in) from the gold card and
9mm ($^3/_8$in) from the green
card. When you are happy
with the effect, fix the layers
in place with double-sided
adhesive tape.

The finished card

The embossed metal jar has been laid first on green card, then gold, then red before mounting on bronze. There are so many possible combinations of metal sheet and embossing powders that this card looks different every time you make it.

These examples were completed using the same stencils, but on card for a completely different effect. Methods of colouring include chalks (this page), chalks on metallic pearlised card (opposite, top), and pigment inks (opposite, below).

Eyelets

by Polly Pinder

Eyelets were a lovely surprise for me. Having used them years ago in the making of belts and children's gym bags, I never thought that they would become part of the card maker's kit.

We card makers are always looking for innovative ideas to embellish our cards and eyelets certainly fulfil that brief. Made from aluminium, they can be practical, decorative or both. It is difficult to believe that something which requires a thoroughly good hammering can ultimately produce a very delicate and intricate design. The manufacturers have designed additional pieces which lie between the paper and the eyelet, representing anything from a Christmas tree to an open hand, an apple, a snowflake or even a tiny birthday cake with candles. These, combined with the variety of papers and card now available, add a fascinating new dimension to card making.

My daughter, in passing, said that she thought handmade cards were little works of art in themselves, and I believe she is right. Time, patience and love go into each one and that is why the recipient always treasures them. As your cards become ever more professional, whether you are making them to send to friends and relations or to sell at a charity fair, do remember to put your name somewhere discreetly so that people appreciate your talents.

I hope you will follow some of the designs in this section and that they will prove an inspiration for you to develop new eyelet ideas of your own.

Polly

Opposite

Flowers are a natural subject for eyelets but they can be put to any number of uses to develop and enhance a design.

Basic techniques

Eyelets could not be simpler to use and you can always release any pent-up frustration by using the hammer! Be sure to buy the correct sized tools to match your eyelets; if the piercing tool is too large, the set eyelet will not have sufficient grip on the card and the eyelet will fall through.

1. Mark where the eyelets will be on your card.

2. Always work on a cutting or setting mat when attaching eyelets. Open the card flat, hold the piercing tool on one of the marks and hammer. One blow should be enough.

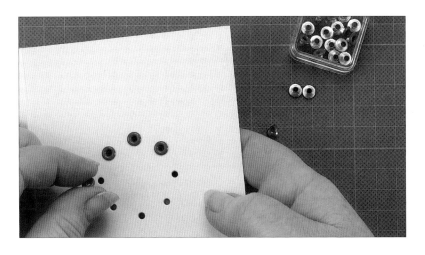

3. Insert the eyelet.

4. Turn the card over and insert the setting tool. One or two knocks with the hammer will curl the tube of the eyelet and press it into the card.

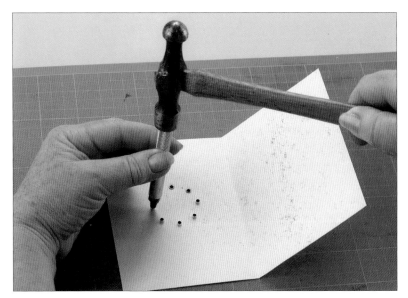

If the eyelet has a decorative piece, lay this over the punched hole before inserting the eyelet.

Heart of Gold

Cut-outs add another dimension to the greetings card. If you haven't used a craft knife for this purpose before, practise on some spare card first. When making internal cuts, the knife really is much easier than scissors.

A heart of gold implies generosity of spirit, so this card need not be restricted to sending only to one's partner – a friend or relation who has shown great kindness would appreciate the sentiment just as much. Should you wish to, there is space in the right-hand corner to write, diagonally in gold, 'Heart of Gold' or simply 'Thank you'. The crinkled foil paper can be bought from most craft shops.

You will need

Cream card blank, 140mm (5½in) square

Cream card, 120 x 135mm (4¾ x 5¼in)

Crinkled gold foil, 100mm (4in) square

Knitting needle and ruler

Craft knife, cutting mat, metal ruler and scissors

Tracing paper and pencil

Eyelet tool kit

One small, plain eyelet and four gold heart-shaped eyelets

Ivory ribbon, 6 x 500mm (¼ x 20in) and darning needle

Clear all-purpose glue and double-sided tape

The template for the Heart of Gold card, shown full size

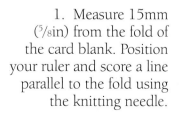

1. Measure 15mm (⅝in) from the fold of the card blank. Position your ruler and score a line parallel to the fold using the knitting needle.

28

2. Trace the three hearts from the template. Position the tracing paper in the centre of the open card (excluding the indented border) and transfer the hearts design. Using a craft knife and cutting mat, carefully cut out the largest heart. Transfer the largest heart again on to the centre of the single piece of cream card.

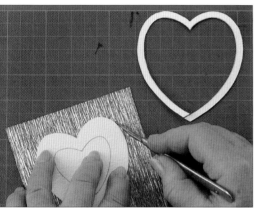

Tip

Crinkled foil is prone to distort. When using a template to cut round, press down very firmly, especially at the edges, and have a really sharp blade in your craft knife.

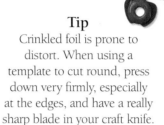

3. Take the triple heart cut from the card blank. Using the craft knife or scissors, cut away to the second heart. Use this as a template to carefully cut out a heart from the crinkled foil.

4. Squeeze a thin line of clear glue round the front of the square of crinkled foil, avoiding the edge of the heart-shaped aperture. Carefully but firmly, press the front of the opened card blank on to the foil.

5. Turn the cream heart over, pencil side down. Glue the foil heart across it so that the crinkles are in the opposite direction to the inlay heart (shown in step 4). Turn the glued heart over and cut out the inner heart shape.

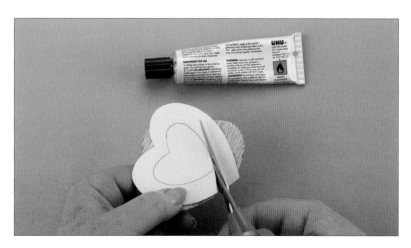

6. Open the card flat and, using the piercing tool and hammer, punch four holes along the indented border. Punch a hole in the small foiled heart in the same way. Insert the small eyelet and set it. Insert the heart-shaped eyelets in the holes in the indented border and set them.

7. Thread 90mm (3½in) of the ivory ribbon through the eyelet in the small heart and glue the ends to the front and inside front of the card so that the heart is suspended in the aperture. Using the darning needle, thread 160mm (6¼in) of the ribbon through the border eyelets. Secure it at the back with small pieces of double-sided tape.

8. Make a bow with the remaining ribbon and attach it using double-sided tape. Run a trail of glue along the inside of the indented border, avoiding the eyelet holes. Press firmly to create a wide spine to the card.

9. When the glue has dried, cut out the large heart shape from the piece of single card and stick it inside the main card to cover the raw edges of the ribbon and foil square.

The finished card is visually quite simple, but it has a lovely, golden-hearted message.

This lovely antique lace veil, circa 1870, is printed on to tissue paper. I found an old paper file almost the same colour, made the card from it and then glued the tissue paper on, leaving the card exposed at the bottom. The tissue paper is available from craft shops but you could try scanning a piece of lace to get a similar effect.

Left: I traced three hearts, slightly overlapping, to make the cut-out shape. The little gold hearts, each cut from striped card at different angles, are strung with gold elastic which is secured at the back with sticky tape.

Right: Handmade paper, incorporating rose petals and leaves, makes a pretty background for threaded ribbon. The little suspended heart was made from the cut-out shape and painted gold to match the eyelets.

Glitter

by Polly Pinder

What can be more magical on a greetings card than some sparkle and glitter and little twinkling areas of colour? Just gorgeous, I love it.

There are some wonderful products available now which enable us to add this enchanting quality to our cards: glittery glues, amazing holographic papers, glinting jewels and lovely, soft, tinsel-like threads. All of these materials have different qualities: they glimmer and glisten, they are bright and shiny, they glow or flash or shimmer. What could be nicer? And in the spirit of the recycling philosophy which now abounds (and which we card makers have been aware of for years), many of the cards in this book have utilised any glittery things which would otherwise have been discarded – used Christmas cards, gift wrap, Christmas crackers, carrier bags, chocolate wrapping and anything I could gather without looking too conspicuously odd! My family are now used to a kind of hovering behaviour; a surreptitious glance at their wastepaper baskets; questioning looks which mean 'You're not throwing that away are you?'. I have even been known to retrieve suitable items from the dustbin, while the family looked on in quiet horror. Never mind; no-one is aware that the cards they so happily receive have very interesting histories.

I hope you will be inspired to follow some of the ideas in this section and perhaps go on to develop your own. Making cards for family and friends is one of the most pleasurable occupations, and long may it remain so.

Polly

Simple designs made special by bits of sparkle. Rubber stamps, old greetings cards, metallic confetti and a used carrier bag have all helped to produce this varied collection of cards.

Flashy Flowers

Like balloons, flowers are a perfect subject for glitter cards because of their general appeal and versatility; they can herald any number of different celebrations.

The exciting element here is the wonderfully changing colour of the pearlescent card. Just hold a piece and tip it slightly one way, then another, and see the orange turn into yellow and green, then bright pink. Amazing! The orange and green cards were originally two small carrier bags.

You will need

Blank cream card, 140mm
(5½in) square

Orange and green pearlescent
cards, 120mm (4¾in) square

Green tinsel thread

Strip of gold glittered card,
25 x 50mm (1 x 2in)

Flower and office hole punches

Craft knife, scissors, circle cutter
and cutting mat

Double-sided tape and 3D
foam squares

Tracing paper, ruler and pencil

Templates, actual size

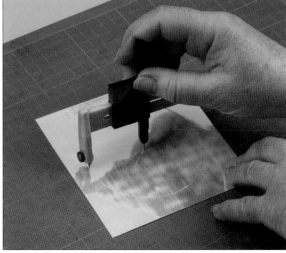

1. Mark the centre of the green square. Adjust the circle cutter to cut a 90mm (3½in) diameter circle. Position the point, and then make the cut.

2. Use double-sided tape to secure the square to the cream card, then transfer the large flower to the back of the circle.

3. Transfer the medium flower and the flower centre to the orange card, then cut out both flowers and the centre.

4. Punch sixteen flowers from the remaining orange card and put a small piece of double-sided tape on the back of each one.

5. Take your ruler diagonally across (corner to corner) and make marks for four flowers. Now find the centre of each side and mark where the top, bottom and two side flowers should be. It will be easy to position the remaining eight after the first eight have been stuck down.

37

6. Stick a strip of double-sided tape on the back of the gold glittered card. Using the office punch, cut seventeen circles. Stick one on to the orange flower centre and the remaining in the centre of each little flower.

Tip
Save a piece of backing from your double-sided tape. Cut a piece of tape to fit the backing. Put the two together. Use an office hole punch to make small circles. These can be used as neat adhesive for punched flowers and other small items.

7. Put four 3D foam squares on the underside of the orange flower and attach it to the green one. Cut four 40mm (1½in) lengths of tinsel thread and position them between the petals using thin strips of double-sided tape.

8. Use double-sided tape to secure the flower centre, and five 3D foam squares to stick the flower on to the card.

Pearlescent, colour-changing card is the dominant element here. The glittering gold flower centres were cut, using an office hole punch, from an old Christmas card. 3D foam squares give depth to the central flower.

Left, top: Here is a gold theme, contrasting matt and shiny textured papers. The fine gold flowers are little outline stickers and the flowers in the bunch were cut using a craft punch. The stems are glitter glue and the blue, magical holographic card was cut from a Christmas carrier bag.

Left, bottom: The same flower shape as used in this project is used again in a single format for this card. Bronze and orange in contrasting matt and shine give an interesting effect. The flower centres are circles of tinsel thread stuck down with double-sided tape. The orange 'jewels' are blobs of glitter glue.

Right: I thought about little flowers hiding in the grass for this card. The colours are unreal, but that's OK. The card itself is a shiny royal blue. Tapering strips of pearlescent card were stuck down, with very fine strips of pink holographic paper stuck on some of them. The flowers were cut from the same paper, some hiding and some raised using 3D foam squares.

Metal & Wire

by Julie Hickey

Some years ago my then boss, Maggie Wright, took me to Dallas to attend a craft trade show. For four days before the show we stayed with her good friend, Vesta Abel, in Tucson, Arizona. During these four days, Vesta introduced me to many new stamping techniques and products. The materials that had me totally hooked were sheets of copper metal. The techniques Vesta used on them were quite simply amazing, and the results fascinated me. Techniques from quilting to embossing could be applied to the metal, and stunning things happened when you heated it. Vesta's work really was art from her heart.

Several years later and again at a craft trade show, this time in Anaheim, California, I met with Jana Ewy. She was using the copper with coloured foil sheets and adding wire accents to her outstanding work. Jana had taken the products to a new level and left me feeling totally inspired.

These two incredibly talented ladies are totally responsible for my love of metal and wire. I have taken all that I have learned from these remarkable ladies and turned it into my own creative projects. I hope you will enjoy them and that they will inspire you to see what you can achieve with metal and wire.

Metal techniques

Rubbing
Found objects can be great to create rubbings from. It is easier with foil than with metal sheets. Place the foil over your found object, such as a shell, and use the wooden tool or embossing tool to rub and trace the patterns and markings on it.

Heating
You can only do this with pure copper. Using a craft heating tool, electric or gas hob or hot air gun paint stripper, heat the metal. It will change from bright copper to burnished orange to pink and then to purple. Finally it goes from blue to silvery gold.

Hammering
Create wonderful texture on the metal or foil by hammering. Use the large end of the embossing tool while resting on the foam sheet, and hammer the metal. Work so that the markings are close together.

Punching
Use different shaped metal cutters to cut out shapes in metal and foil.

Embossing
Use the embossing tool to create patterns on the metal or foil with a foam sheet beneath your work to help absorb the pattern.

Crimping
Feed the metal or foil through the rollers of the crimper to create a fabulous corrugated effect.

Wire techniques

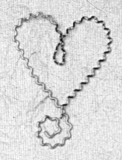

Crimping
Feed the wire through the rollers on the crimper, and hey presto! Beautifully crimped wire. This works best with 22g or 26g wire.

Hammering
Once you have bent and shaped some wire, you can use a hammer and anvil to give your work a beaten look. This works best with 18g and 22g wire.

Winding and wrapping
I have used 26g wire to wrap around metal and foil. I found it easier to attach the end of the wire to the back of the piece with double-sided tape before beginning.

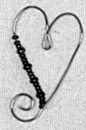

Beading
I used seed beads when wrapping my work, so I needed 26g wire. If you use bigger beads, you could change to 22g wire.

Sparkle
Add glitter glue to a piece of shaped and beaten wire to give extra sparkle and lift to your work.

Bending and shaping
Round-nosed pliers are great to start the bending and shaping of the wire, then let your fingers take over. This works well with 18g, 22g and 26g wire.

Burnished Daisy

This daisy card is an easy project to get you started. Using just a few techniques, you will start your creative journey into metal and wire cards. You will learn to cut, trace, emboss and heat the copper metal to create this stunning card. Having made this daisy card, you will be filled with confidence to continue your card making.

You will need

Copper metal (1 sheet)

Card: A4 size black, fuchsia and purple

Scissors

Pencil • Plastic eraser

Tracing paper

Embossing tool • Foam sheet

Heating tool • Chopping board

Double-sided tape

Craft knife • Cutting mat

Metal ruler

Paper trimmer

Heating tool safety

Always heat metal on a heat-proof surface such as a chopping board. Remember that the metal conducts the heat, so if you are holding it with your fingers, keep them well away from the area you are heating. You can hold the metal with a wooden peg to be absolutely safe.

The pattern for the Burnished Daisy card

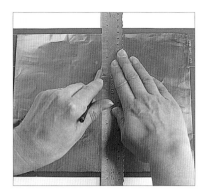

1. Cut the copper to size with a craft knife and metal ruler, on a cutting mat. You can also use scissors. The design is $10.5cm^2$ ($4^1/8in^2$), but leave some space around the edges.

2. Trace the pattern. Lay the tracing on the copper and place the copper on a foam sheet. Emboss the pattern using the medium point of an embossing tool.

3. Put the embossed copper on to a heat-proof surface such as a chopping board. Heat the copper with a heating tool and watch as the colours change.

4. Heat the copper all over until it turns a burnished orange colour. As soon as the area you are heating turns this colour, move on to the next part.

5. Next, direct the heat on to specific areas to change the colour further. After the orange, the copper turns pink.

6. Heat the squares in the corners of the design until they turn silver.

Using the heating tool
Hold the heating tool 2.5cm (1in) away from the copper sheet when heating it.

8. Apply double-sided tape to the back of the copper. Cut a 11cm^2 (4^3/$_8$in^2) piece of fuchsia card. Peel back the ends of the backing paper from the double-sided tape, and place the copper on the fuchsia card.

7. Cut round the design using a craft knife and metal ruler on a cutting mat. Be careful as the edges of the copper can be very sharp.

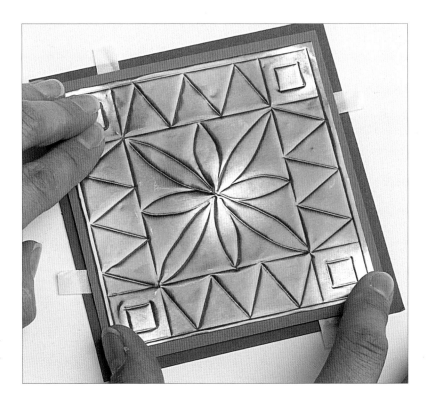

9. Cut a 12cm^2 (4^3/$_4$in^2) piece of purple card and mount the fuchsia card on it in the same way.

10. Mount the purple square on your black card, which should be cut to 26 x 13cm, (10^1/$_4$ x 5in) and scored and folded to make a 13cm square.

Two of these cards were made using only part of the daisy pattern: one features the central flower, another uses two borders placed together. The card on the far right has a similar border, but shows different patterns created using the embossing tool. Don't forget to decorate your envelopes to match.

Polymer Clay

by Candida Woolhouse

I have always loved shapes and colours. Some of my earliest toys are still fresh in my memory; in particular, I can remember the feel of the wooden diamond pieces from a mosaic set, their bright colours and the satisfaction of slotting them neatly into place. If you are the sort of person who regularly arranges your coloured pencils into a rainbow inside their tin (so they look good enough to eat each time you open it), then you think like me!

This desire to play with shape and colour has never left me and it has found an outlet in numerous crafts over the years. Significantly, out of all the craft phases I have gone through: knitting, painting, scale model aircraft, jigsaw puzzles and modelling with anything from paper straws to matchsticks, polymer clay has lasted the longest. This may have something to do with the fact that, with polymer clay, you are master of both shape and colour. It has to be the most versatile craft medium I have ever used, as well as one of the simplest.

My first dabblings with clay came about while I was living in the British Virgin Islands. Although the lifestyle there is simple and uncomplicated, I could never go long without wanting to create something with my hands, and working with clay satisfied this urge. What caught my imagination and sparked my interest was an example of a millifiori cane in a children's craft book. I was fascinated by the potential of such a technique, not least because I always loved finding out how things worked – and this is the way the traditional English confectionery rock is formed!

I launched straight into cane work and used the results to cover foil armatures in the shape of dolphins, shells and starfish which made ideal Christmas tree decorations. The Caribbean also had to be the perfect place to go crazy with loud colours! The vibrancy of nature's colours in the tropics is unique; the sea an unimaginable array of azure blues, teal and ultramarine, whilst the flowers are saturated with intense hues of every shade. These bright colours are reflected in the card designs I chose for this section.

It may be clay, but you do not have to be a skilled sculptor to produce some fantastic results. Greetings cards are a great beginning, providing as they do a miniature canvas on which to work. I hope that the simplicity of my designs are apparent and that they will convince even the most timid craftsperson to give it a go.

Candida

Festive Snowman

Making this happy snowman should increase your confidence in working with clay. The simple act of twisting two contrasting colours into a rope is an effect you could use in many other designs. The shape of the card is novel, which is just what a home-made card deserves to be!

You will need

White, black and red clay

Craft knife

Ruler

A4 (8¼ x 11¾in) sheet of black card

Silver gel pen

Glitter glue

Large and small silver star sequins

All-purpose glue

PVA glue

Cotton wool

1. Use white clay to make a body shape. Roll a ball of clay for the head, flatten it slightly, stick it on the body then use the craft knife to cut off the top of the head.

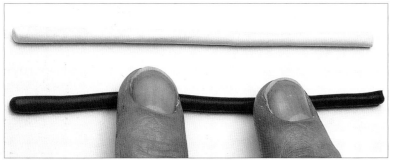

2. Roll two long thin logs for the scarf – one white, one red.

3. Twist both logs together.

4. Roll the twisted log down to the final diameter. If necessary add more twists, then roll again.

5. Cut the ragged end off the log and attach the cut end to the side of the snowman's neck. Drape the scarf across the body then carefully cut it to length. Alternatively, cut the scarf to length before attaching it to the body.

6. Attach the other part of the scarf in a similar manner, then use the clay shaper to smooth the ends and neaten up any dents in the body.

7. Roll two balls of black clay – one 10mm ($^3/_8$in) diameter, one 6mm ($^1/_4$in). Flatten the large ball to form a disc, then cut through the disc slightly to one side of centre. Discard the large part.

8. Turn the small part of the disc so that its cut edge faces downwards and attach it to the top, flat part of the head to form the brim of the hat. Flatten the small ball of clay slightly, then press this on to the brim to complete the hat.

9. Complete the snowman by making indentations and adding the eyes and nose. Bake the model in the oven.

10. Working from the left-hand side of the sheet of black paper, mark two fold lines 9cm (3½in) apart, then score along these lines with the back of the craft knife. Fan fold the card, then trim off the excess from the right-hand side of the paper.

11. Open up the card, use a silver gel pen to mark the start, middle and end positions for a wavy line across the front two panels, then draw a wavy line through these marks.

12. Cut the card along the drawn wavy line and up the side of the back panel, then refold the card.

13. Glue the silver star sequins on to the three layers of the card, taking the small stars down behind the cut edges of the front two layers.

14. Apply a layer of glitter glue along the top of the cut edges, then set the card aside to dry – preferably overnight.

15. Glue the snowman on to the front flap of the card.

16. Finally, use PVA glue to secure the cotton wool 'snow' under the snowman.

The finished card and a matching gift tag

Father Christmas

I combined the use of cutters with hand modelling to produce the desired effect for this card in a neat and easy fashion. The beard is the most complex part of this design; I used two different sizes of carnation flower cutters, but you could use fluted circular or oval cutters. I moulded the rest of the face and added the pompom on his hat for extra interest.

Candle

The original idea for this card sprang from a lovely glittery flower stamen that I found in a haberdashery shop which made an ideal flame for the small candle featured on the gift tag. The scale was too small for the card itself, but the glitter glue applied around a clay flame adds the necessary sparkle!

Christmas Crackers

Once again, the idea for this card came by chance. I came across a small cracker cutter and I just had to use it! I worked up a rough design, but the shapes were too small for a card, so I turned it into a gift tag. To make the larger crackers for the card I hand cut the shapes from rectangular strips of flattened clay, and rounded them over smaller tubes of clay before baking.

Christmas Pudding

For me, this is a graphically satisfying design. I used a plain circle cutter to make the pudding shape. I used a large flower cutter to create the scalloped shape of the white sauce, then cut into this with the circle cutter so that the two parts fitted neatly together. The currants are small balls of clay.

Silk Ribbon Embroidery

by Ann Cox

Experimenting and developing new ideas is enormous fun, but when I started this section I had absolutely no idea the hours of pleasure I would have doing it. I was allowed to develop ideas and techniques from silk ribbon embroidery and simplify the methods of working to make them suitable for card making. The projects are small and therefore quick to work, so why spend hours searching for a card with that extra something when you can create one that is original and really personal?

First and foremost I am a silk ribbon embroidery designer and without doubt this is my first love. I only work with silk – its characteristics make it easy and quick for the embroiderer to shape each individual stitch. The only stitches I have worked for the cards in this section are ribbon stitch, straight stitch, lazy daisy stitch and gathering stitch in ribbon and couching and fly stitch in thread, but I have used new and different techniques to create this wide variety of flowers for you to choose from. All of these cards work on both fabric and card and you do not need to use an embroidery hoop. I also show you how to paint the ribbon to increase the range of flowers that can be worked.

At the start, make sure you have an envelope to fit the finished card. It is infuriating when finished to find there is no envelope to fit. Keep the project simple – avoid having too many fussy bits and pieces and above all keep the work impeccably clean.

As you turn the pages of this section I hope you will be tempted. There are lots of new ideas and techniques to make card making easier and give a more professional finish. Use these ideas and never be afraid to experiment to create your own original cards.

Happy sewing!

Thread stitches

Couching: A single strand of toning thread is used to secure another thread in place. This is useful when working curved stems.

Fly stitch: This is a single open looped stitch similar to a lazy daisy stitch. It is often worked as a calyx for flowers such as rosebuds.

Opposite
A selection of the beautiful cards that can be made by embroidering with silk ribbon without using an embroidery hoop.

Three Irises

Lazy daisy stitches are perfect for the irises in this project and may be worked in any combination of colours.

Many flowers can be created by embroidering silk ribbon directly through card without the use of fabric. However, not all flowers can be worked this way, since the stitches need to be far apart, otherwise the card will collapse. Flowers with many petals worked to a centre must have a hole in the card with a piece of fabric at the back to support the stitches.

When I embroider directly into card, I always mount the embroidered card just above the base card using silicone, to add to the dramatic effect.

It is fun to have a session using off-cuts of card and pieces of silk ribbon. Experiment with different stitches and colours –the results will be useful if a card is needed in a hurry!

You will need

Red single-fold card blank, 14 x 10cm (5¾ x 4in)

White textured card, 15 x 10cm (6 x 4in)

Fancy-edged scissors

Glue stick

Mapping pin and foam mat

Needles: two size 18 (medium) chenille and one crewel size 8

Green coton à broder

4mm (⅛in) silk ribbon: 25cm (10in) each of purple (177), blue (117), red (02) and yellow (15) and 1m (39½in) of deep green (21)

Clear silicone sealant

The pattern for the Three Irises card. Photocopy it to make a template.

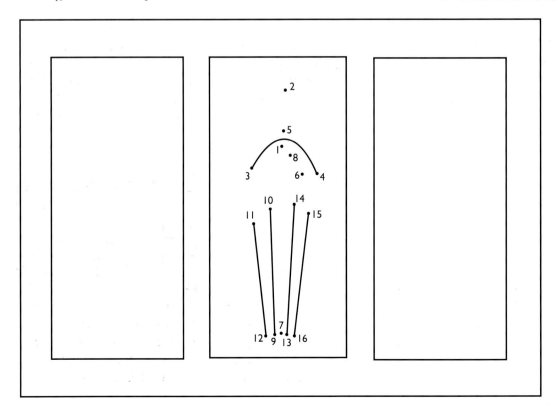

62

1. Use the fancy-edged scissors to cut three 3 x 8cm (1¼ x 3⅛ in) panels from the white card. Use the mapping pin to transfer the design on to each panel. Working on the first panel, anchor the 4mm (⅛in) purple ribbon at 1 then take the needle back down through 1 again.

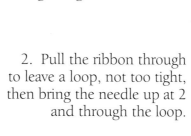

2. Pull the ribbon through to leave a loop, not too tight, then bring the needle up at 2 and through the loop.

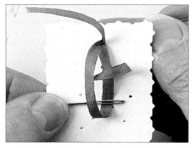

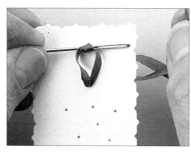

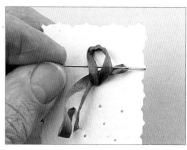

3. Pull the ribbon through. Take the needle over the loop and back down through at 2, using the eye end of a second needle to keep the ribbon flat.

4. Pull the ribbon through, keeping the loop tight against the needle as it is pulled through, so that it spreads the loop and sits neatly over the top.

5. Remove the second needle, bring the ribbon up through 3, then use the eye end of the needle to take the ribbon under the first loop.

6. Take the ribbon down loosely through 4 and back up at 5. Be careful not to stitch through ribbon at the back.

7. Pull the ribbon through then take it down through hole 6. Anchor the end and snip off any excess ribbon.

8. Use the mapping pin to make a new hole through the ribbon and card, one-third down the last loop.

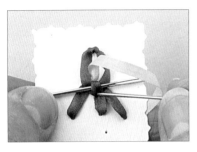

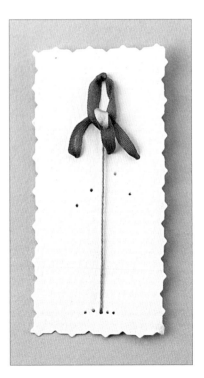

9. Bring the yellow ribbon up carefully at 5, then, using the eye end of a second needle under the purple ribbon loop to support it, take the yellow ribbon needle down through the purple ribbon and the new hole in the card.

10. Pull the ribbon through, trim off the excess and anchor the end on the back of the card.

11. Make a new hole 8, just below the centre and concealed behind a petal and work a straight stitch stem using green coton à broder, coming up at 7 and down at 8. Fasten off.

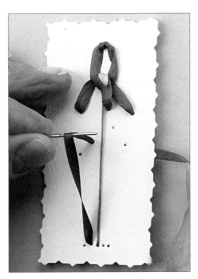

12. Anchor the green ribbon at 9 with a touch of glue.

13. Turn the card face up, re-thread the green ribbon and take it down at 10. Use the eye end of a second needle to create a twist in the ribbon and keep it tight over this needle as it is pulled through to the back.

14. Bring the ribbon up at 11 and then down at 12, adding a twist as in step 13. Continue working to make two more leaves from 13 to 14 and 15 to 16 then anchor the end on the back.

15. Now complete the other two panels, then use silicone to place the panels slightly raised on the red card blank.

The finished card with a matching gift tag. Irises come in every colour imaginable, in one shade as I have shown here or a combination of two colours. Try using a different tone or shade for the lower petals – experiment and have fun.

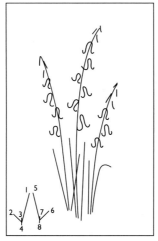

These templates for the cards shown opposite are all printed half size, so you will need to enlarge them 100% on a photocopier.

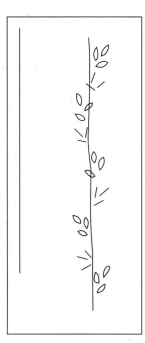

angle of needle

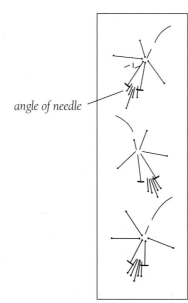

Clockwise from top left:

Daffodils

The petals are worked with 4mm($^1/_8$in) ribbon in pale yellow (13), yellow (15) and gold (54); the trumpets with 7mm ($^1/_4$in) yellow and gold ribbon and the leaves with 2mm ($^1/_{16}$in) moss green (20) and deep green (21) ribbon. Start with the back petals, anchor a yellow ribbon at 1 and a toning thread at the back. Bring the thread up at 2, lay the ribbon round the thread and take the thread over it and back down to hold the ribbon. Bring the needle up again at 1, secure the ribbon to complete the first petal, work the remaining petals, then fasten off. Use 7mm ($^1/_4$in) yellow ribbon to work a centre ribbon stitch trumpet using a second needle as on page 12. Add stems and leaves.

Apple Blossom

Prepare the card and draw in the stem, then partially unravel a 5cm (2in) length of string and stick with PVA for branches. Using 7mm ($^1/_4$in) pink (08) and pale pink (05) ribbon, work each straight stitch petal from the centre to the tip. Work ribbon stitch leaves in various greens with 4mm ($^1/_8$in) and 7mm ($^1/_4$in) ribbon. Use one black and five yellow threads to work the stamens.

Three Fuchsias

Using a mixture of 7mm ($^1/_4$in) pinks (24, 25, 166), red (02) and mauve (177) ribbons, start at 1 and work the bell with two straight stitches. Now complete the fuchsia.

Bluebells

Work the straight stitch stem and couch the top to curve. Flowers are two offset lazy daisy stitches with a few tiny straight stitch buds at the top. Start with the lowest and work up the stem. Use 4mm ($^1/_8$in) moss green (20) ribbon for the straight stitch leaves.

Climbing Rosebuds

These rosebuds are tiny lazy daisy stitches using 4mm ($^1/_8$in) dusky pink (163) ribbon. Avoid taking ribbon across the back of the work. Anchor off after each group of stitches is worked. Lay the stem on the surface and couch in position. With two strands of green thread, work a straight stitch from the centre to the base of a bud and then a fly stitch for the calyx. Work ribbon stitch leaves with 4mm ($^1/_8$in) green ribbon.

Card & Thread

by Polly Pinder

One of the lovely aspects of card and thread is that the structure of each threaded shape can look extremely complex, as if it must have taken hours of painstaking work to create, but once the simple technique has been mastered, stunning threaded shapes can be quickly and easily produced.

Some readers may remember a craft called 'pin and thread', in which rows of shiny-headed nails were banged into pieces of wood, then threads of string, wool, cotton, raffia or fine wire were wound round the nails to produce spectacular images. Card and thread is very similar. The principle is the same: the act of winding thread to create an image, but nails and pins are not required. Instead, notches, Vs or slits are cut into the card shape, then thread is wound round the shape and is caught and secured in the notches. A pattern is created, with the design governed by how many notches, Vs or slits are missed during the winding process. It sounds much more complicated than it is: once you get winding there'll be no stopping you, and the design possibilities are endless.

There are many beautiful papers and cards available to complement your card and thread designs: they come in all textures and shades and can be chosen from craft shops or picked up wherever you see them: I have used an office folder and a chocolate box lid whilst preparing cards for this section.

Striking new metallic threads are now available in a variety of plies and textures, and there are silky and satin threads in a multitude of colours, or multicoloured ones that vary in tone, all just waiting to be wound intriguingly into the shape of a flower, a cat or butterfly.

I have always believed that a beautifully handmade greetings card, created with patience and love, is equal to any expensive gift. It will always be treasured by the recipient. I hope that the step-by-step projects and the other cards shown in this section will generate enthusiasm and inspire readers to create many wonderful card and thread images.

Polly

Basic techniques

The technique of card and thread is to wind the thread round the back and front of a card shape, catching it in slits, Vs or notches to secure it. Variety is achieved through the colour, texture and thickness of the thread, the distance between the slits and the number of slits missed when threading.

Transferring designs on to card

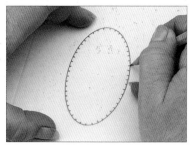  

1. Trace the design straight from the book or enlarge or reduce it on a photocopier to the size you require.

2. Turn the tracing paper over, place it on your card and go over the lines again with your pencil.

3. Cut carefully around the basic shape.

Cutting the card's edges

Threads are available in fine, medium and thick. The three cutting methods shown below can accommodate the varying degrees of thickness and texture in a thread. Metallic foil thread can be rather slippery and springy, so a slit in the card traps it more securely than a V or notch.

You can cut slits around the edge with a craft knife, on a cutting mat, or use very sharp, pointed scissors.

For thicker thread you will need V- shaped cuts, which can also be made with a craft knife or with sharp, pointed scissors such as nail scissors.

You can cut notches with deckle-edged craft scissors. You will need to practise to ensure that you end up with a balanced number of cuts ready for winding.

Winding

Winding involves securing the thread at the back of the shape, catching it in a notch, then taking the thread across the front of the card and missing a certain number of notches before catching it again. The thread is then wound round the back and up to the notch on the right of the starter notch.

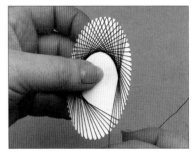

1. Secure the thread to the back of the card shape using a small piece of sticky tape. Take the thread to the edge, catch it in one of the notches and turn the shape over.

2. Miss however many notches are recommended in the project. Here I missed nineteen and caught the thread in the twentieth, then caught the second notch and the twenty-first, then the third and the twenty-second.

3. Continue wrapping the shape in this way until all the notches have been threaded.

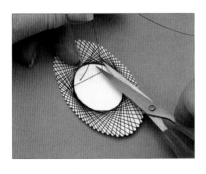

4. When the winding is complete, secure the thread at the back with another small piece of sticky tape and cut off the end.

Tip
Some metallic threads have a mind of their own and spring out of the V shape when the winding reaches a particular point. To avoid this, keep securing the thread at the back.

Winding is started by catching the thread in the first notch. These different effects are created by varying the number of notches that are missed before catching the thread again. The more notches that are missed, the smaller the central hole will be (see the shape on the left). If the thread is taken directly across a shape at its halfway point, as in the middle shape, there will be no hole. If only a few notches are missed, as in the right-hand shape, the hole will be quite large.

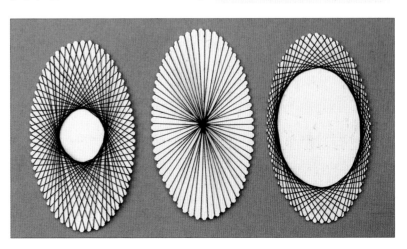

Flower Power

I chose a lovely, shiny, multi-shaded thread for the flowers on this card and used two strands. Beads play a significant role in the design. The really tiny seed beads in the centre of each flower are available from most craft shops. They are secured to circles of card using double-sided tape. The larger beads are slightly different from each other in shape and colour. The whole design is unified by the use of varying shades of a single colour: in this case, pink.

You will need

Card blank made from blue card, 100 x 210mm (4 x 8½in)

Same blue card, 100 x 210mm (4 x 8½in)

Medium thickness, multi-shaded pinkish thread

Very tiny pinkish seed beads

5 each of 3 different shapes of larger bead in various pinks

2 x 150mm (6in) craft pipe cleaners, pink

Tweezers and scissors

Sticky tape

Double-sided tape

Clear all-purpose glue

Tracing paper and HB pencil

Craft knife and cutting mat

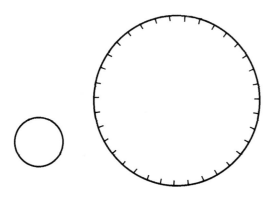

The templates for the Flower Power card

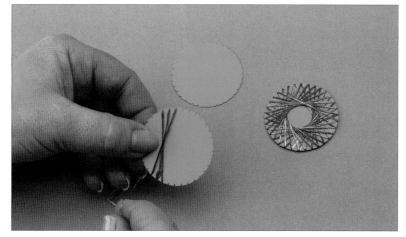

1. Trace the large circle and transfer it three times on to blue card. Cut out the three circles. Using your cutting mat and craft knife, cut a V shape at each pencil mark round the edges.

2. Secure the thread at the back of a circle with a piece of sticky tape and catch the thread in the first V to begin winding. Leave twelve Vs empty and catch the thirteenth. Then go round the back to the second and across to the fourteenth and so on. Secure the end of the thread with sticky tape and cut the thread. Repeat with the other two circles.

3. Trace the smaller circle, transfer it three times on to blue card and cut the circles out. Squeeze a blob of glue on to one circle. Using tweezers, carefully position five of the larger, matching beads. Leave to dry for ten minutes, while repeating with the two remaining circles and two sets of beads.

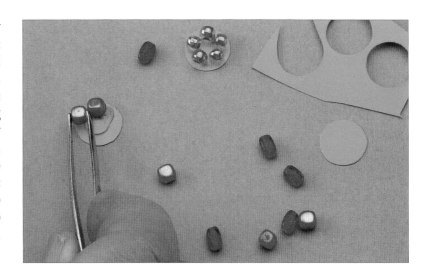

4. Transfer three more of the smaller circles on to part of the remaining card. Stick a strip of double-sided tape to the back of the card, behind the circles. Cut the circles out.

Tip

It is much easier to apply the double-sided tape before cutting out the shapes.

5. Tip the tiny seed beads into a shallow container. Remove the backing from the double-sided tape. Place the circle sticky side down in the beads and press firmly so that as many beads as possible become attached.

6. Stick a beaded circle on to the centre of each threaded flower using a blob of glue or a piece of double-sided tape.

7. Cut a narrow strip of double-sided tape slightly shorter than one of the pipe cleaners. Stick it along the bottom of the card about 10mm (½in) from the edge. Remove the backing and attach the pipe cleaner to the sticky strip.

8. Cut the other pipe cleaner into six different lengths. Cut strips of double-sided tape to match the pipe cleaner lengths. Attach the strips of tape to the card, peel off the backing and secure the pieces of pipe cleaner, pressing down firmly.

9. Attach each flower head to a stalk using either a blob of glue or double-sided tape. Press firmly to secure.

Your choice of materials can make all the difference to a design: here a natural feel is created by the subtly variegated thread and tiny seed beads in pinky copper shades. The chunky pipe cleaner stalks, beaded flowers and bold shapes add to the fun feel of the card and thread technique.

The feathers for the sparkly, rather exotic-looking card on the far left were cut from a feather duster, but they are available from most craft shops. They were stuck to the card using a combination of all-purpose glue and sticky tape. Two gold threads were used: a fine one for the petals and a much thicker one for the flower centre. A flat-backed gemstone makes a stunning decoration.

The toned purple flower was built up to give a three-dimensional effect using 3D foam squares. Fibrous handmade tissue paper was stuck on to the card using a glue stick.

Highly textured paper is a dominant feature of the card on the right. The flowers, like the components of the purple flower, were cut out using deckle-edged craft scissors.

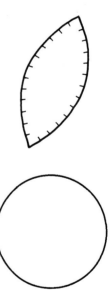

The threading template for these cards. The top one makes the petals for the card on the left and the leaves for the one on the right. The circle should be cut out using deckle-edged craft scissors to make the notches for the purple and pink flowers.

Quick Parchment Craft

by Janet Wilson

The cards in this section feature a cross between simple embossing techniques and paper pricking borrowed from the original, more time-consuming parchment art form. This section looks at making parchment cards using a basic kit and three-step stencils and suggests ways of mounting your finished pieces as attractive cards. You will learn how to colour the parchment paper prior to embossing as well as how to spot colour areas of the embossed project, using permanent marker pens and coloured pencils. Ideas for freehand decoration of the projects are shown, and how you can devise your own designs by using only parts of the stencils.

For the more adventurous, I suggest more advanced ways of using the stencils, and introduce a couple of basic decorative techniques from the original parchment art form.

If you enjoy the projects and really get hooked, perhaps you will want to go further and try your hand at the original, ancient art of making parchment cards. In the meantime, enjoy using these simple techniques to make beautiful handmade cards.

Opposite
A selection of cards showing the many different ways the stencils can be used. Embossing, pricking and colouring are combined with decorative techniques borrowed from the original parchment art form.

Basic techniques

Making a control piece

The stencils used throughout this section are three-step stencils, two of which are normally for embossing. The third may have a combination of further embossing and perforating work, or may be solely for perforating. I recommend that you make what I call a control piece for each of the sets of stencils you purchase and keep it with the stencils. The control piece shows all the embossing and perforating areas contained on the three-step stencils. When you have made it, you can decide which lines you need not emboss for your project and which parts of the perforating you want to use or leave out. This piece is also of great assistance when you want to change the direction of, say, a piece of ribbon when you start experimenting with more advanced projects using the stencils.

This demonstration shows you how to make a control piece using the bow stencils.

You will need

Basic kit plus Bow three-step stencil

Parchment paper 14.5 x 9.8cm (5¾ x 3⅞in)

Low tack tape

Dual-tip medium/small ball embossing tool

South American style hard embossing mat

Ruler with a grid

Dye inkpads and cosmetic sponges

Scrap card

Permanent markers

Flat no. 4 paint brush

Coloured pencils and blender pencil

Plastic eraser

Large estralina

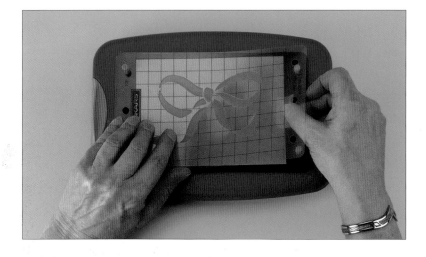

1. Position a piece of parchment underneath stencil 1 and tape it to the mat using low tack tape. You can turn the base when embossing or perforating so that it is in the best position for you.

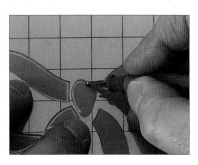

2. Emboss the areas on stencil 1 using the medium embossing tool. Plastic stencils are prone to move while you are working, so keep your fingers on the stencil to hold it still.

Tip

If you are using normal weight parchment, you do not have to press hard when embossing. Apply a similar pressure to that which you would use with a pencil.

3. Emboss the areas on stencil 2 in the same way.

4. Perforate with stencil 3 using the perforating tool. Always keep the tool upright when perforating.

The finished control piece. Keep this with the three-step stencils so that you can see at a glance what effects are produced by all the stencils.

Tip

When using the perforating tool, you only need to break the surface of the paper. If you push the tool down too far it will 'bruise' the parchment, leaving a white mark, and you will also distort the hole on the stencil.

Stippling and using white pencil

Normally the control piece would be kept for a reference, but here I have decorated it in order to demonstrate two further techniques.

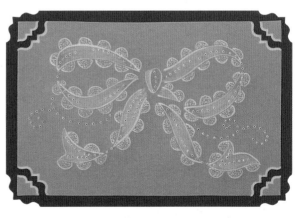

1. Put the parchment on the hard embossing mat or a cutting mat and using the perforating tool, stipple the half-moons along the ribbon edge. Gently bounce the tool up and down.

2. Turn the parchment over and using a white pencil, shade the ribbon area. This will give the design light.

The finished piece. To mount the project, I cut a piece of dark paper measuring 6mm (¼in) more all round than the parchment. A photo corner punch was used on each corner and the parchment was slipped in and secured using small pieces of sticky tape on the back. Spray adhesive or double-sided tape could be used to adhere this layer to the base card.

Cross hatching

This method of decorating parchment projects is used in South America. It is easy to do and the resulting pattern can be decorated in various ways. I recommend using a hard embossing mat for this work.

  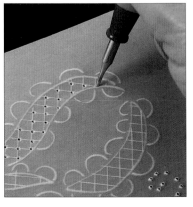

1. Working on the back of the parchment and using a ruler with a grid and the perforating tool, emboss parallel lines across the ribbon. Do not press too hard.

2. Turn the parchment round and starting in the middle, cross hatch with lines at right angles to the first lines. The grid on the ruler will help.

3. Place the parchment, right side up on the perforating mat and use the perforating tool to make holes where the lines cross.

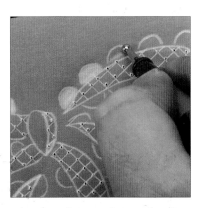

4. Turn the parchment over. Using the embossing tool, rub each of the half moons with a back and forth motion.

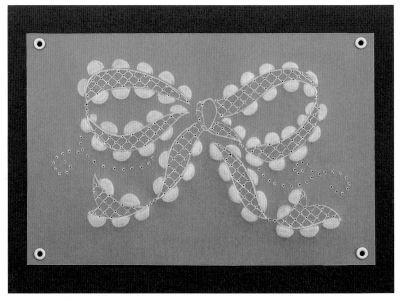

The finished piece. This time the parchment project has been attached to the base card using eyelets. Parchment work shows to better advantage on a dark background like this.

Colouring parchment

Sometimes you may want to use coloured parchment or add colour to areas of the design to give a different effect to your work. Here are some methods that I use.

Using inkpads

The ink from dye inkpads dries fairly quickly, and is easily applied to the back of the parchment using a cosmetic sponge. You can make the colour paler by wiping off excess ink. Check what the colours look like from the right side of the work.

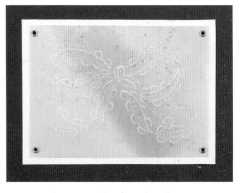

1. Place the parchment face down on a scrap of card. Using a cosmetic sponge, dab on blue ink. Any excess ink can be wiped off using a clean sponge.

2. Dab on red ink using a fresh sponge. It is a good idea to label your sponges with the ink colour so that you do not mix them up!

The finished card. I have added a third colour, then mounted the project on to a pale coloured layer, which shows the coloured parchment better, and attached it to the base card using eyelets.

Spot colouring

This is another easy way of adding a little colour. I use permanent markers as they dry quickly. The colour is applied to the back of the project so remember to check the appearance from the front, which will be different.

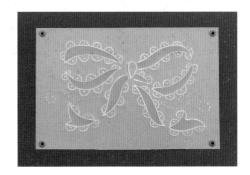

1. Place the parchment face down. Using a pale blue permanent marker, colour some of the ribbon.

2. Add dark blue and before the ink dries, blend the colours together using a flat no. 4 paint brush.

The finished card is attached to a dark, toning coloured base card using eyelets.

Colouring with pencils

Adding colour to your projects using coloured pencils is the method favoured in South America and some delightful effects can be achieved quite simply. Apply light strokes of the pencil to the back of the parchment, starting with the palest and moving on to darker colours. Check the appearance from the front. Any excess colour can be removed with a plastic eraser. After that you can use the blender pencil to blend colours. This does tend to make colours slightly darker.

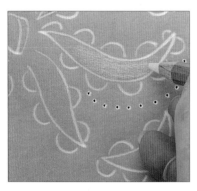

1. Use a pale blue coloured pencil first.

2. Then use a dark blue pencil, overlapping the pale blue slightly.

Tip

You can always rub out mistakes with a plastic eraser.

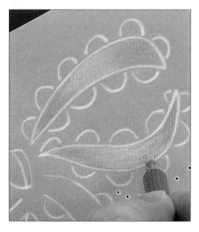

3. Use a blender pencil over the whole area to smooth out the pencil marks.

4. On the hard embossing mat, use the large estralina on the back of the parchment to make a circle in each half-moon.

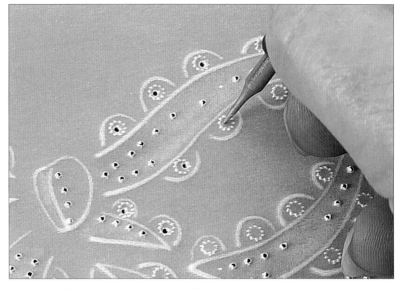

5. Lay the parchment, wrong side up, on to stencil 3 and pierce the pattern in the ribbons using the perforating tool.

6. Turn the parchment the right side up and pierce a hole in the middle of each estralina circle.

The finished card

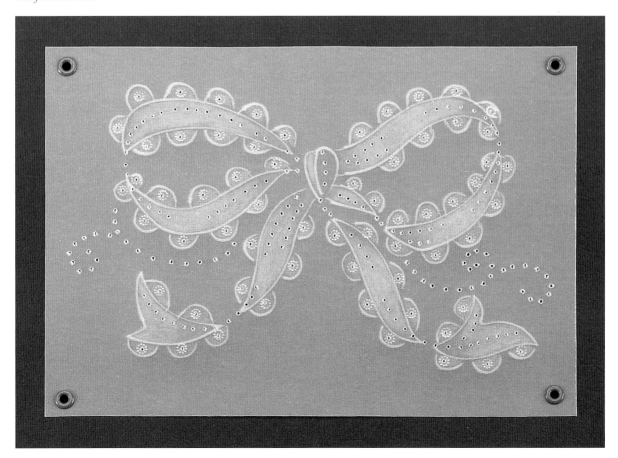

Beautiful Butterfly

Butterflies are always popular subjects for card makers as they come in all different sizes, shapes and colours. Parchment gives you an even wider range of ways you can depict them and use them in your card making.

You will need

Basic kit and the Butterfly three-step stencil

Dual-tip medium/small ball embossing tool

White pencil

Large and small estralinas

Fun foam mat

South American style hard embossing mat

Perforating grid

A5 parchment paper

Permanent markers in three colours of your choice

Ruler with a grid

Medium circle hand punch

A4 off-white card

Dark blue metallic paper, 12 x 12.5cm (4¾ x 5in)

Four blue eyelets

Eyelet kit

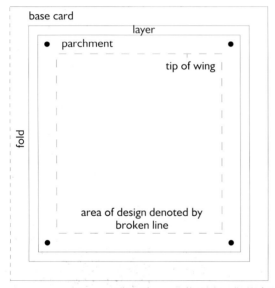

The pattern for the Beautiful Butterfly card, shown half size. Enlarge it on a photocopier.

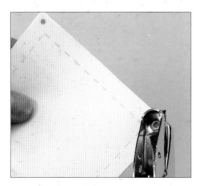

1. Photocopy the pattern. Cut the parchment to 11 x 11.5cm (4⅜ x 4½in). Using the photocopied pattern as a guide, punch four holes with the circle hand punch.

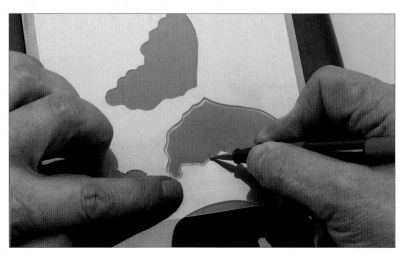

2. Position the parchment under stencil 1. Emboss with the medium embossing tool.

86

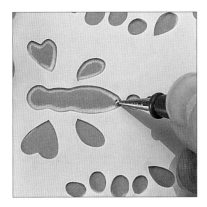

3. Change to stencil 2 and emboss the body and the four shapes beside it.

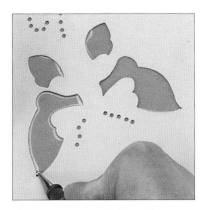

4. Using stencil 3, emboss the wing shapes.

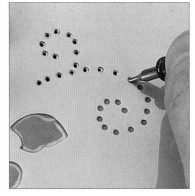

5. Working on the fun foam mat, use the same stencil and the perforating tool to pierce the curlicues.

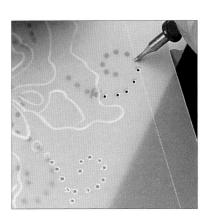

6. Move the parchment and position it over the same stencil to add extra pierced curlicues to each side of the wings.

7. Working on the back of the parchment, colour in areas of the butterfly using three different permanent markers.

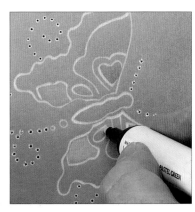

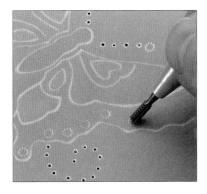

8. Use the large estralina to make circles along the inside edges of the wings, and add one at the tip of each antenna, one just below the body and four in a row along the body.

9. Use the small estralina inside the large estralina circles at the tip of each antenna, and along the body. Add a small circle below the large circle beyond the end of the body.

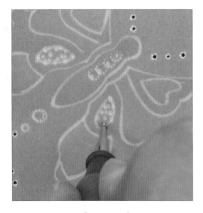  

10. Using the medium embossing tool, add dots to the tear shapes on the wings, and at the centres of the estralina circles at the edges of the wings and along the body.

11. Cross hatch the area shown using the perforating tool and a ruler with a grid.

12. Use the perforating tool to make freehand crosses where the cross hatched lines intersect. Press down gently.

13. Secure the parchment over the perforating grid and perforate the areas shown.

Opposite

The finished Beautiful Butterfly card. Use the pattern, enlarged on a photocopier to full size, as a guide to punch the eyelet holes in the parchment and the dark blue paper layer. Cut the off-white card to 28 x 14.5cm (11 x 5¾in) and fold it in half. Punch eyelet holes in the front of the card only. Using the eyelet kit and four blue eyelets, secure the parchment and blue layer to the card.

The all-white effects give this uncoloured parchment a lacy look, and the design, with its row of smaller butterflies on one side has a slightly oriental feel to it.

Top: Some areas of the wings have been coloured using permanent marker, and the Puerto Rican straight edge cutting tool has been used round the outside edges of the wings so that they can be raised slightly after the project has been mounted. The Puerto Rican scallop cutting tool adds a decorative edge to the parchment.
Bottom: The large butterflies have been created by using the stencil and then reversing it. The edges of the small butterflies' wings have been perforated to give them a slightly raised appearance.

Glass Painting

by Judy Balchin

Handmade greetings cards and gift tags are always fun to make and a delight to receive. Many of my relatives and friends have actually framed cards that I have made, which is a compliment to me as well as a continuing pleasure for them.

The title of this section may seem a little worrying, so let me explain: no glass is actually used for the cards featured. The section shows how glass painting techniques can be used on clear acetate, which is then mounted on, or framed by, card. Whether you are a beginner, or an old hand looking for new ideas, you should find something to interest you. Anyone new to glass painting will find it an inexpensive way to sample the delights of this fascinating hobby.

The projects are planned to take you on a slow and enjoyable learning curve, introducing new techniques as you progress. Techniques covered include outlining and painting; diluting the glass paints to achieve more subtle pastel effects; the production of 'mosaics', and the creation of shaped and window cards. From simple but stylish to outrageously glitzy, you should find inspiration in these pages.

Most of the designs are relatively simple. The bold outlines filled with vibrant, transparent colour can stand alone or can be enhanced for that extra sparkle. The designs and techniques can be adapted to create fridge magnets, mobiles or bookmarks, or worked on glass to make pictures, decorate plates and vases, and much more.

Part of the fun of creating your own masterpiece is browsing through the wonderful array of backing cards and papers available, and choosing coloured gems, glitter or other items for decoration. You can keep your cards simple, or make them as ornate as your imagination allows. My main problem is knowing just when to stop!

As you work through the section, your glass painting skills will develop. Try combining elements, taking a border from here, a motif from there, to create a new design. Do not discard ideas as you experiment with the outliners and paints: what can at first seem a mistake may spark off something new and exciting. I hope that by sharing my techniques and flights of fancy, I have provided a launch pad for your own ideas. Glass painting is both therapeutic and addictive. I should know: I have been doing it for ten years and am still enjoying every minute. My best advice is to enjoy your hobby. Have fun!

Opposite: a selection of handmade cards.

Mother's Day

What mother would not be absolutely delighted to receive a beautifully-painted basket of flowers on her special day? This project shows how to make a cut-out card, which makes the flowers look even more convincing.

Sometimes, especially when there is no light shining through the acetate, glass paints can look a little dense. This project uses glass paints which have been diluted to produce a more pastel effect. The paints should be diluted with a clear, glass painting medium or with varnish. Do not use water or white spirit, and if in doubt ask your local craft shop.

You will need

White card 13 x 16cm
(5⅛ x 6¼ in)

Acetate sheet slightly smaller
than the card

Glass paints: pink, purple,
green and clear

Palette

Scissors

Masking tape

Paintbrush No.4

Pencil

Scalpel

Cutting mat

Spray adhesive

gift tag template

Full-size template

94

1. Fix the design to thick white card using masking tape. Secure the acetate over the design and outline it carefully. Leave it to dry.

2. Pour a little clear glass paint into a palette and add a few drops of pink glass paint. With your paintbrush, mix the paints together gently to avoid creating air bubbles.

3. Use the diluted pink glass paint to paint half the tulips.

4. Make a mix of diluted purple glass paint and use it to paint the rest of the tulips. With a diluted green glass paint mix, complete the leaves and stems.

5. Paint the basket with diluted yellow glass paint, applying it more thickly in some areas for a more intense effect. Leave to dry.

6. Cut round the design using small scissors.

7. Score the white card down the middle, and fold. Cover the reverse of the design with spray adhesive and place on the front of the card, butting it up to the fold.

8. Open the card and place it on a cutting mat. Use a scalpel to trim off any excess card from around the outlines of the flowers.

9. Close the card and use a pencil to draw the outline of the flowers and leaves on to the inside back panel of the card.

10. Following the pencil lines, use a scalpel to cut off any excess card from around the outlines of the flowers.

The finished card and gift tag

Templates

Note

The card templates on this page have been reduced in size. To use, photocopy with the setting at 162 per cent.

gift tags - full- size

Tea Bag Folding

by Kim Reygate

I first became involved with papercrafts at a needlecraft show in 1996. Rubber stamping looked fun and, after attending a series of classes over the next few months, I became a self-confessed 'stampaholic'. My addiction, however, did not stop with stamping and I went on to try many other papercrafts, including tea bag folding.

So what is tea bag folding, I hear you ask. It has little to do with soggy wet tea bags, it is simple origami using small decorative squares of paper. The origins of this papercraft lie in The Netherlands where tea bags were enclosed in pretty paper envelopes which were then used as the basis for creating beautiful rosettes – hence 'tea bag' folding. Tea bag papers, papers printed with small square designs, are now available specifically for this papercraft.

I started teaching tea bag folding in 1998 and I soon became known as the 'Bag Lady' because I always arrived at my classes laden with lots of bags. I have since played with, and taught, just about everything to do with stamping and papercraft but my regular students still think of me as the Bag Lady from those first tea bag folding classes.

I hope that the projects I have created show you that inspiration can come from anywhere. Just about any type of paper can be used to create a square, which can then be folded and transformed into wonderful rosettes. In fact I ran out of space for all the ideas that were racing around in my head when compiling this section.

I do not throw anything away because there will always come a time when I might need that little scrap of 'waste'. As I strive to use up all those little left-over pieces, I am constantly reminded of something said by one of my mentors – 'It's never a mistake, it's always an opportunity'.

I hope that these words inspire you in the same way.

Kim x

Basic folds

Just three basic folds are used to make all the projects in this book: the square, the triangle and the kite. The only skills required are cutting the squares accurately and making crisp-edged folds. Master these folds and you can create a kaleidoscope of different designs. A single design of printed tea bag square can produce four different patterns from each type of fold. When the folds are assembled, each pattern will produce two different rosettes; one by placing the folds left over right, the other by placing them right over left. When you have mastered a fold with tea bag squares, try folding squares cut from other types of paper – a random design in each square can create a stunning finish.

Square fold

This is probably the easiest fold to start with and it will lead you on a journey of discovery. You will need eight identical tea bag squares.

1. Start by folding a paper, side to side.

2. Use a bone folder to crease the fold.

3. Open the paper, then fold and crease the other sides.

4. Open the paper, turn it over, fold corner to corner, then crease the diagonal.

5. Open the paper, then fold and crease the other diagonal.

6. Open the paper and check the folds.

7. Turn the paper over, then using the creases as a guide, start to close the fold.

8. Flatten the paper to form a small square. Repeat steps 1–7 with the other seven papers, ensuring that each square has the same design at the front.

9. Apply a dab of all-purpose adhesive.

10. Insert another paper snugly inside the first so that the bottom points are aligned. Here I am assembling the folds left over right.

11. Close the fold, and press the glued pieces together.

12. Repeat steps 10–11 with the other six papers to complete the rosette.

One design of tea bag square can create four different square folds, each of which can be assembled to produce two different finished rosettes.

The open sides of the square folds in the left-hand column were trimmed with deckle-edged scissors before being assembled (see page 104).

Triangle fold

This fold is made by reversing the steps used for the square fold on pages 102–103. It is probably the most versatile of the three folds in that, with a little modification, it can be used to create non-rosette shapes. You will need eight identical tea bag squares and deckle-edged scissors to trim the open edge of each triangle fold.

1. Fold a paper corner to corner. Use the bone folder to crease the diagonal (see page 102).

2. Open the paper, then fold the other corners together and crease the diagonal.

3. Open the paper, turn it over, then fold it side to side.

4. Fold and crease the other sides, then open the paper and check the folds.

5. Close the folds to form a triangle, ensuring that your chosen image appears on the front face. Repeat steps 1–5 with the other seven papers.

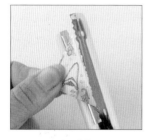

6. Use deckle-edged scissors to trim the open edges of the fold. This neatens any uneven folding.

7. Referring to page 103, apply a dab of adhesive to one fold, then insert a second fold snugly inside the first. Ensure that the bottom points of the folds are aligned.

8. Close the fold, and press the glued pieces together. This example shows a left over right assembly.

9. Repeat steps 6–8 with the other six papers to complete the rosette.

One design of tea bag square can create four different triangle folds, each of which can be assembled to produce two different finished rosettes.

The open edges at the top of the folds used in the right-hand column were trimmed with deckle-edged scissors before being assembled (see page 104).

Kite (or nappy) fold

This fold is slightly more complex than the square and triangle folds, not in the folding, but in the assembly of the rosette. You will need eight identical tea bag squares. The folds must be assembled at the correct angles (see step 8) so that they form a tight circle. Any deviation will make it almost impossible to perform the final manoeuvre, and a lopsided or buckled rosette will result.

When using printed tea bag squares it is essential to decide which of the four corners is to form the points of the rosette; the first fold must be made through this corner.

1. Fold a paper corner to corner through your chosen top point.

2. Open the paper, take one of the sides across to the fold line, then carefully crease along this diagonal.

3. Repeat with the opposite side to form this shape.

4. Fold the bottom point up as shown.

5. Open the fold, turn the paper over, then fold up the bottom point along the crease made in step 4. Repeat steps 1–5 with the other seven papers, ensuring that same design appears on each fold.

6. Turn the paper over and apply a small dab of adhesive to the right-hand corner of the fold as shown.

7. Turn the paper over again and insert the glued corner in the top of the centre opening of a second kite fold...

8. ...then carefully slide the paper down until it is positioned as shown. Working clockwise, repeat steps 6–8 to assemble the other six kite folds.

In this demonstration the kite folds were assembled right into left. If you want to assemble the folds left into right, apply the adhesive to the left-hand corner in step 6.

9. To attach the last fold to the first, turn the rosette over and dab adhesive on to the exposed corner of the last fold...

10. ...turn the rosette over again and carefully bring the last fold to the front...

11. ...then slide the glued corner of the last fold into the opening of the first.

One design of tea bag square can create four different kite folds. Each variation of fold can be assembled left into right or right into left (see steps 6 and 7) to produce two different finished rosettes.

The two top sides of the folds used for the rosettes in the right-hand column were trimmed with deckle-edged scissors before being assembled (see page 104).

Terracotta Tiles

Getting just the right colour of card or paper can make or break a project and so when all else fails, I make my own. A combination of butterscotch, terracotta and cranberry dye based inks have been used to create both the paper on which the tea bag images have been stamped and also the background to the finished card. This technique is a particular favourite of mine, but can be quite messy, so you might want to wear plastic gloves.

You will need:
A5 (4¼ x 5¾in) single-fold white card

Two sheets white paper, cranberry-coloured paper and black glossy card

Gold border craft stickers and tweezers

Rubber stamp cube, butterscotch, terracotta and cranberry dye-based ink pad

Fine and coarse sponges

Clear embossing powder and heat tool

Clean-up pad or baby wipes and paper towel

Rotary trimmer or craft knife, metal ruler and cutting mat

Southwest corner punch

Bone folder

DSST

1. Use a fine cosmetic sponge and butterscotch ink to apply colour randomly to the sheet of white paper.

2. Now sponge terracotta ink randomly over the butterscotch ink.

3. Change to a coarse sea sponge, then apply a random pattern of cranberry ink.

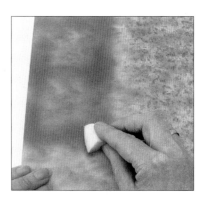

4. Use the fine cosmetic sponge and terracotta ink to create two 8cm (3in) squares of darker colour at one end of the sheet.

5. Use cranberry ink and the stamp cube to stamp eight square images at the stippled end of the decorated sheet. Leave a small gap between each square.

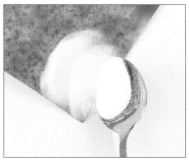

6. Use cranberry ink to stamp another image then, while the ink is still wet, quickly spoon on some clear embossing powder.

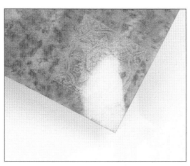

7. Gently tap the paper to shake off the excess embossing powder…

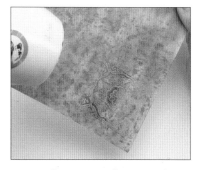

8. …then use a heat tool to set the embossed image. Leave to cool.

9. Using a craft knife, carefully cut away the corners of the embossed square. Retain the corner pieces for use as decoration in step 18.

10. Referring to pages 106–107, use the other eight squares to prepare a kite-fold rosette.

11. Tear a sheet of scrap paper in half to leave a rough edge (here, yellow paper is used for clarity).

12. Temporarily secure one half of the paper to the front of the single-fold card.

13. Sponge the exposed part of the card (see steps 1–3), then use the stamp and cranberry ink to create a random pattern.

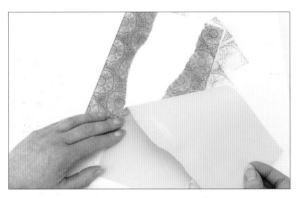

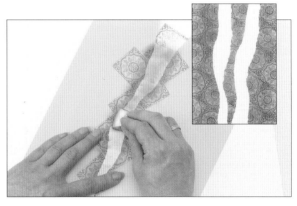

14. Repeat step 13, using the second piece of the scrap paper to create a similar random pattern on the other side of the card.

15. Now use both pieces of paper to create a pattern through the middle of the card.

16. Corner punch two 6.5cm (2½in) squares of cranberry paper, use DSST to attach them to slightly larger squares of black card, then trim this to leave a narrow border. Attach the squares to the dark area on the sponged sheet, then trim to leave a border all round.

17. Attach the rosette to one of the squares prepared in step 16, and the trimmed embossed shape to the other.

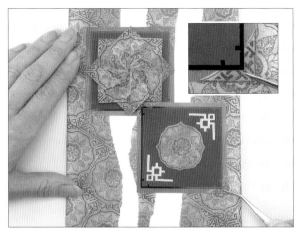 

18. Attach the two squares to the card, apply decorative corner-shaped craft stickers as shown, then, using tweezers, carefully glue two of the pieces trimmed off in step 9 to each of the decorated squares.

19. Finally, cut some small squares from the sponged sheet and attach these to the white spaces on the card.

The finished card, together with matching envelope and gift tag.

Sea Treasures

An unusual rubber stamp cube with beautiful seaside images inspired me to create this card. I combined embossing with pale blues to give a wonderful seaside feel.

Spring Fever

I used printed tea bag papers to make the kite-fold rosette on this card. Before assembling the kite folds, I trimmed round the flower shapes at the top of each fold to create a completely different finish.

I mounted the rosette on a layered octagonal panel, the colours of which echo those on the tea bag papers.

Bugs

The wonderful stamped and embossed bugs on the square panel of this card were coloured with pearlescent paints.

This kite-fold rosette was made using squares cut from some of my own handmade background papers. I did not want the rosette to overshadow the bugs, so I used a smaller square punch than usual to make the tea bag squares.

Peel-Offs

by Judy Balchin

Birthdays, anniversaries, weddings, seasonal celebrations ... they are all perfect excuses for making those extra-special cards. The delight of receiving a handmade card can only be outweighed by the enjoyment to be gained from making one. These days it could not be easier, thanks to peel-off craft stickers. These sheets of stickers come in a wide range of colours and themes, are amazingly easy to use and give a truly professional finish to your cards. Your only problem will be how to choose just which of the hundreds of designs to use. Flowers, animals, borders and corners, lettering, frames, wedding and birthday designs and much more – the list seems endless!

Cards can be simple, or they can be embellished with handmade papers and jewels. Matching gifts can be created too – these stickers may be delicate in appearance, but they are surprisingly tough. They will stick to plastic, glass and even wax, and will adhere to flat and curved surfaces. So now it is time to begin. You are about to embark on a journey of fun and creativity, and I hope you enjoy it as much as I have done. Bon voyage and happy sticking!

Judy.

A selection of handmade cards made using the methods shown in this section.

Stick and Sprinkle

This is such a fun technique, I could not resist including it! The craft sticker is pressed on to transparent adhesive foil and then sprinkled with coloured sand. The sand sticks to the film, not to the sticker. It is great fun choosing colours and creating different patterns with the sand. I have used sand in fresh floral colours to create the 'garden' seen through the silver window.

You will need

Silver window-shaped peel-off craft sticker

Silver border craft stickers

Silver flower craft stickers

Coloured sand: I used purple, pink, green and white

Transparent self-adhesive foil 14 x 11cm (5½ x 4¼in)

Cream card 10 x 13cm (4 x 5in)

Scalpel

Soft brush No. 8

Scrap paper

Teaspoon

The sticker

1. Peel the protective backing from the self-adhesive foil.

2. Lift the window sticker, let it rest for 30 seconds to regain its shape, and lay it on the self-adhesive foil.

3. Cut round the window shape.

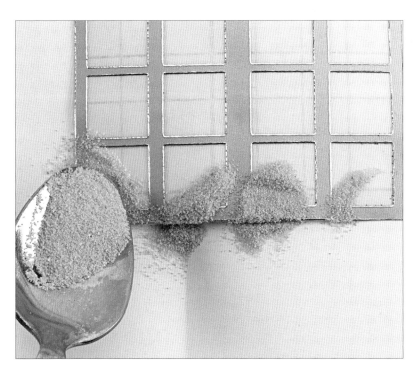

4. Lay the shape on a piece of scrap paper and use a teaspoon to sprinkle some green sand carefully on to the design to represent the foliage.

5. Tap the excess sand off the card on to the paper and replace it carefully in its bag.

6. Repeat with purple sand, then with pink, to represent the garden flowers.

7. Add some more green sand for the trees.

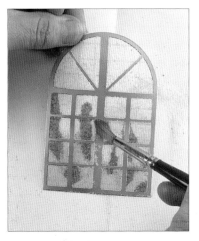

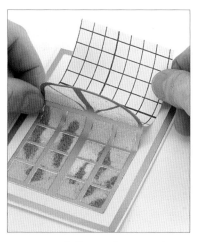

8. Sprinkle the remaining area with white sand. Brush away any excess sand.

9. Cut strips of border and press them on to the edge of the card.

10. Carefully peel away the backing sheet and stick the sanded design to the card.

11. Decorate the corners of the card with silver flower stickers.

Opposite: the finished card. Decorate the finished window card and gift tag with small silver flower stickers.

Create sanded backgrounds to mount your decorated craft stickers on. Coloured glitters, applied in the same way as sand, also look stunning when they are combined with silver or gold stickers.

Rubber Stamping

by Melanie Hendrick

I believe that within all of us there is creative potential waiting to be discovered or rediscovered and nurtured.

Some of my favourite creative memories are of making cards – for family, friends, overseas relatives on their birthdays, or to say 'thank you' or 'I miss you'. A greetings card can say so much, but a handmade card can say so much more.

I discovered the wonder of rubber stamping on a cold and windy Saturday afternoon. A few days before, I had started a new job, and had been handed a pack of blank cards, a rubber stamp and a multi-coloured inkpad. 'Go home and make some cards', I was instructed. Making cards was fine, no problem, but what was I supposed to do with this wooden block with a rubber image adhered to it? Over the years, I had printed from potatoes (when I was six) and from hand-carved lino, but I had never heard of rubber stamping before. To me, stamping was something the Post Office did!

With some curiosity, I picked up the stamp and inked it with the multi-coloured inkpad, and stamped a sunflower on to a piece of card. Wow! Like a woman possessed, I stamped every piece of card I had, plus envelopes, and even the pages of my diary – anything I could get my hands on. I was hooked.

My enthusiasm hasn't waned since. As you turn the pages of this section, you will discover that rubber stamping opens up a whole new creative world. The humble blank card has been replaced with wonderful textures, vibrant colour and even decorated matchboxes! Nothing is unstampable when you have a little know-how.

I have heard rubber stamping described as good therapy and highly addictive, and I agree – what a wonderful and healthy way to spend your time! So put aside any fears or household chores, order takeaway for the family and join me on a creative adventure full of discovery and lots of fun.

Happy stamping!

Melanie Hendrick

Treasure Chest

I get a buzz out of creating cards that are more than cards. This treasure chest is what I call a gift card: the concertina card mounted on the lid opens to reveal a message, whilst the drawer has room for a tiny gift inside – perfect as a little thank you gesture, or just to say 'I saw this and thought of you'. After being stamped with permanent ink, the chest and card are sponged with a succession of colours to create an antiqued effect. It's great fun to work small and the card is collaged with tiny decorations.

Tip
Permanent ink is used in this project as it dries very quickly, and paint can then be sponged on top of it.

You will need
Small matchbox
Permanent black ink
Daisy and sun stamps
A5 white card
Acrylic paints
Sponges
4 wooden beads
Gift for inside
Double-sided tape
Black card
Gold mesh
Gold metal
Creative punch: circle
Glue
30cm (12in) cord or ribbon
Seed beads
Ruler
Bone folder

1. Take a matchbox, open it and split the lid. Turn the matchbox inside out, since acrylic paint binds better to the untreated surface. Ink a sun stamp with permanent black ink and stamp the design. Do the same with a small daisy stamp, as shown. Stamp the base of the matchbox in the same way.

2. Take an A5 sheet of white card, and stamp both sides in the same way as the matchbox. Choose four acrylic paints: two earth tones, a teal blue and a purple. Put some colour on to a sponge and pat down on the flattened matchbox lid, over the stamped images. Then wipe over the painting with a sponge. Apply the lighter earth tone first, then the darker one. Use a separate sponge for each colour. Wiping creates an antiqued effect.

3. Take the blue teal colour, sponge on and wipe with the clean end of the sponge.

4. Fold up the lid a little and sponge purple paint on to the edges. Repeat the whole sponging process on both sides of the A5 sheet, over the stamping, and on the base of the matchbox.

5. Assemble the box, re-attaching the lid with double-sided tape where it was originally glued. Put a gift inside – this is the accent from a necklace. Glue four matching beads to the bottom of the matchbox lid. These will be feet. Do not glue them to the matchbox itself, or you will not be able to get the lid on again!

6. Measure the length of the matchbox – this one is 7cm (2¾in) long. Cut the decorated A5 card to this width. Then measure the width of the matchbox, and mark this measurement along the length of the decorated card, top and bottom. Use a bone folder and ruler to score and fold according to these marks, to concertina the card.

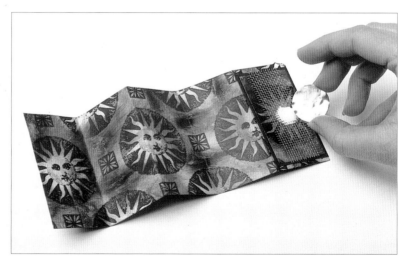

7. Cut a piece of black card 1cm (½in) shorter than the matchbox. Then cut a piece of leftover decorated A5 card ½cm (¼in) smaller all round than the black card. Use double-sided tape to stick both pieces to the end of the concertina, as shown.

8. Cut a piece of gold mesh the length of the black card but 1cm (½in) narrower. Glue it on. Punch a circle of gold metal using a creative punch and glue this to the mesh.

126

9. Punch out a circle from the decorated A5 card, showing the face of the sun (use the punch upside down). Flip the sun over and tear towards you to make a smooth tear down the centre of the face. Glue half of the face to the gold circle.

10. Cut out two of the daisy designs from the leftover decorated A5 card, and stick them to the top and bottom of the mesh. Glue a seed bead to the centre of each daisy.

11. Apply double-sided tape to the last page of the concertina, top and bottom. Place the cord centrally across the matchbox lid, and hold it in place with double-sided tape as shown.

12. Peel off the backing of the double-sided tape. Fold up the concertina, position it on the lid and press it down. You can embellish the outside of the lid with beads. Tie the cord in a single knot.

Tip
This cord is handmade but any cord or ribbon can be used.

Opposite
Experiment with different shapes and sizes of matchbox. The clock treasure chest has the rubber stamp used for the clock design inside it as a gift. The tiny blue and purple chest has a musical score design stamped in gold on the concertina card. The cord on the black and white chest unties to reveal a spiral design in silver wire. Pearlescent beads are used as an accent on the orange and purple chest, completing its stunning oriental look.

The gift inside the finished treasure chest was taken from the same necklace as the beads used for feet. The message can be written in metallic gel pens or glitter pens on the back of the concertina card.

Watercolour

by Jane Greenwood

In my thirty years as an illustrator I have always kept watercolour painting as a valued hobby. For my work I use inks for their permanence. The joy of watercolour, by contrast, is its spontaneity: rather than planning rigidly how you are going to paint a subject, you can let accidents and surprises happen – like the little fish in the aqueous painting at bottom left. Here, washes used with salt looked like a marine landscape, so I added fish to complete the picture. Surprises like this make ideal artwork for cards.

Many things in this section are made up. Simple forms with imagined colour schemes can be turned into an effective card by simply cutting them out and mounting them on coloured card with a frame or line border in a complementary colour.

The lemons were painted from life, and I have shown how you can add drama and interest to such paintings by adding a striking patterned background to the lemons, traced from a scarf.

I do hope this section will inspire card makers who have been discouraged by watercolours due to the impression that they are too difficult. Don't be put off! Following these simple steps, you will quickly get the knack and appreciate their ease and rapidity of use. I hope that the watercolourists who buy this book will also be inspired by the ideas shown. Good luck and I hope you enjoy yourselves as much as I did when making the cards for this section.

Jane A Greenwood

Basic techniques

A graduated wash

This is the first thing you learn when getting accustomed to watercolours. A wash is used mostly for backgrounds but can be the subject of a painting, too. In this case we are making a graduated wash to look like a sky.

You will need

Small watercolour pad, 300gsm (140lb)

Brushes: no. 12 and no. 6 round, flat

Watercolours: Prussian blue, viridian, cadmium yellow

White gouache

Toothbrush

Salt

Natural sponge

Masking fluid

White candle

1. Mix Prussian blue with three times as much water. Take the no. 12 brush and brush across the paper in horizontal strokes from the top downwards, adding more water as you reach the bottom. Never go back over the wet paint.

2. Tip the paper to accentuate any effects you desire as the paint spreads into the water.

Spattering

The basic wash looked like a seascape to me, so I added some rocks and sea spray to create a feeling of movement. You can spatter using a paintbrush or a toothbrush.

Tip

Practise both techniques first so that you can control the direction of the spatters.

Load the brush with white gouache and flick the brush diagonally across the paper. Keep the brush at least 7.5cm (3in) from the paper.

A toothbrush can be used if you want the spatters to spread freely over a large area.

Wet in wet

This technique involves dropping colours into a wet wash. Surprising effects can occur when colours are mixed in this way and one spreads slowly into the other.

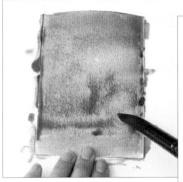

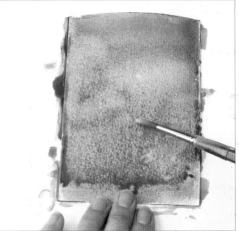

2. Take the smaller brush and drop a mix of cadmium yellow in to the lighter areas of green. Clear water can also be dropped in to lighten the washes.

1. Using the larger brush, paint a wash of Prussian blue. Then load the brush with viridian and drop the green into the blue. Watch the colours spread and mix.

Using salt

While washes are very wet, you can experiment with salt crystals which create unusual patterned effects.

1. While the washes are wet, sprinkle salt on the paper and watch the effects begin as the paint dries.

2. When dry, the salt can be removed using a dry brush.

3. I decided that the salt effects produced during this demonstration looked like a marine landscape, so I lifted out a couple of fish shapes with a clean, dry brush.

Lifting out

Once you have created a graduated wash, you can invent a landscape by lifting out paint to create a cloudy sky or simply by lightening the horizon to suggest the sea. You could also add a field or a beach in this way.

1. Using a small sponge, soaked in water and squeezed out, lift out cloud shapes from the wet wash. Roll the sponge over so that you are using a paint-free area each time.

2. Take a small, flat brush and drag it through the still wet wash two-thirds of the way down the painting, to suggest a horizon.

Masking

You can paint a simple image with masking fluid, either on white paper or on top of a light wash. Then paint a wash over it. When the wash is dry, the masking fluid can be rubbed off with your finger and a startling white image or an area of lighter wash is saved. This can be left as it is, painted in another colour or given form using shadow and tone.

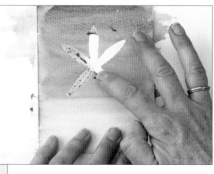

3. When the wash is dry, rub off the masking fluid with a clean finger.

1. Paint a simple shape using masking fluid and an old brush. Wash out the brush immediately.

2. When the masking fluid is dry, wash over the top with Prussian blue. Thin the wash at the bottom of the painting.

Wax resist

A candle or a piece of candle can create a resist over which to paint in watercolour. This is quicker but less precise than using masking fluid.

Tip
Direct a strong light on to the paper while using the candle so that you can see what you are drawing.

1. Use a white wax candle to draw a simple design.

2. Apply your wash over the candle wax and the design will appear.

You can cut out the paintings with fancy-edged scissors or paint a wavy frame around them. Mount them on card in a contrasting colour or tone.

Lemons on Blue

A still life is a useful subject to paint as domestic objects sitting around the house can easily be arranged into a pretty composition, and then with an unusual way of framing or mounting they can be jazzed up to look fresh and original. When I had painted these lemons, I though they looked a little boring so I made up a table cloth by tracing a patterned scarf. The wavy lined border is where I ran out of pattern!

You will need

Smooth watercolour block, 250gsm (90lb)

No. 6 round brush

Cadmium yellow, lemon yellow, yellow ochre, Prussian blue, ultramarine blue, alizarin crimson

Dark blue card, 286 x 205mm (11¼ x 8in)

Pencil and putty eraser

White candle

White gouache

Paper tissue

Tracing paper

Craft knife and cutting mat

Spray mount

1. Arrange three lemons as shown and sketch them from life. Take a candle and 'draw' highlights with it on the lemon drawings.

136

2. Painting from life, wash lemon yellow over the whole area of the lemons. The highlights will remain white because of the wax resist from the candle.

3. Mix yellow ochre with a tiny bit of Prussian blue to paint the shadowed areas.

4. Mix a little Prussian blue and lemon yellow to make green and paint this around the mound at the end of the foreground lemon.

5. When the painting is dry, add details using cadmium yellow mixed with yellow ochre and ultramarine blue. Allow to dry again.

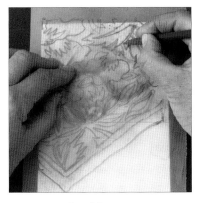

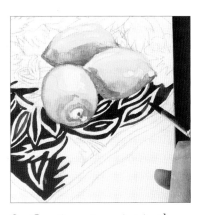

6. Trace the fabric pattern and transfer it on to the painting, leaving a gap for the lemons.

7. Mix ultramarine blue and alizarin crimson and begin to paint the fabric pattern using a no. 6 brush.

8. Continue to paint in the pattern, turning the paper around as you go so that you don't smudge your work. Load the brush with paint and let it sit on the paper.

9. Paint the finishing touches and allow the painting to dry.

10. When the painting is dry, take a brush wet with clear water and sweep it across the patterned area around the lemons to suggest shadows from gentle creases in the fabric.

11. Blot the wetted paint with paper tissue to suggest highlights.

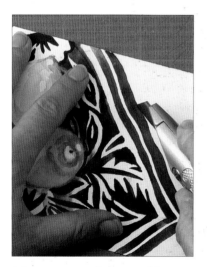

12. Remove the pencil lines from around the point at the bottom of the fabric with a putty eraser. Using a craft knife and a cutting mat, cut around the point.

13. Turn the painting over and apply spray mount lightly to the back. Always work in a well-ventilated room when using spray mount.

14. Take your sheet of dark blue card and score and fold it in half. Stick the painting to the front of the card. Paint a white line all the way round, just beyond the edge of the painting, using white gouache.

The purply blue background is complementary to the yellow lemons, making a pleasing combination for a really striking card. The asymmetric framing takes the design out of the ordinary.

Introducing patterns can enliven still life subjects. You can also achieve this by cutting a composition in two and using only half of it – dare to be different! The sculptural quality of shells, and their subtle, natural colours make them fascinating to paint.

Beaded Cards

by Patricia Wing

There are so many techniques you can use for card making, and using beads, gems and lace with pricking and embossing techniques will considerably add to your repertoire.

There is a wealth of templates available for pricking out and stencils for embossing, to help create that extra special card. Most templates and stencils are a pleasure to work with, as someone has already created the design – you only have to follow the pattern, so pricking out or embossing could not be easier.

Stitching on beads adds another dimension, as do all the lovely gems. Beautiful lace will also complement the beadwork and you will be surprised at the originality you can achieve by cutting out designs from within the lace.

Although your cards will take longer to complete if you add these techniques, you will feel that the finished work is well worth all the effort. You can, of course, design your own beaded cards but pricking out the design first really helps with stitching on the beads.

The Victorians produced some extraordinarily beautiful cards, which form an important part of the heritage they bequeathed to us. Equally, the cards you create could become future family heirlooms that your family will cherish in years to come.

Keep an eye open for inexpensive jewellery – old earrings and brooches often have attractive glass gems that will enhance your work and make it unique. You can find all sorts of things in charity shops, and locally I visit an auction house where boxes of broken jewellery and oddments can yield a treasure-trove of embellishments for my cards!

Pat Wing

Opposite
These cards show some of the effects that can be created using beads, gems, pricking and embossing techniques and lace in your card making.

143

Basic techniques

The techniques used to make the cards in this section, such as embossing and pricking, are easy to learn and perfect for beginners. You will be amazed at the beautiful cards you can make with a few simple techniques.

Punching shapes

Craft punches are a fantastic asset to card making – you just punch out the pattern, which could not be easier. Often you can choose to layer the shapes as punch patterns come in several different sizes.

1. Place the paper in the punch.

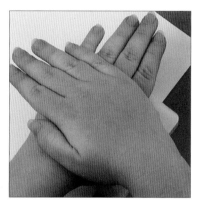

2. Press down firmly to cut through the paper.

3. The punched paper falls out underneath the punch.

Craft punches come in all shapes and sizes, and as shown here you can often punch the same shape in several sizes.

Pricking out

When pricking out to give a decorative pattern, the finished design can have a flat or a raised finish. These are achieved by pricking through your card either from the front (flat) or the reverse (raised).

1. Tape the template to the back of the card using masking tape. Pricking from the back creates a raised effect.

2. On a mat, use a pricking tool to prick through the holes in the template.

3. Peel off the tape and turn the card over to reveal the pattern.

The same design pricked from the front gives a flatter, softer effect.

Gluing on beads or gems

A fine-tipped PVA glue applicator makes it very easy to apply the smaller gems to your work – there is nothing worse than surplus glue!

1. Use a fine-tipped PVA glue applicator to place dots of glue where required.

2. Use a cocktail stick with a tiny bit of glue on the end to pick up a gem and place it on a glue dot on the design.

3. Press the gem with the other end of the cocktail stick to secure it.

The finished design.

Embossing with a light box

Embossing is done from the back of the card with a rounded tool which pushes the card into the pattern of the stencil. This gives an elegant, raised finish on the front of the card.

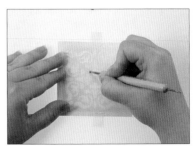

1. Using masking tape, fix the stencil to the centre of the light box. Switch on the light.

2. Tape the card over the stencil, right side down.

3. Press the embossing tool into the pattern as required.

4. You can select all or only part of the stencil pattern to suit your card design. When it is finished, peel off the tape and turn the card over to see the design.

Sewing on beads

This technique requires the template to be taped to the face of the card to give a flat finish, and you only need to prick through very lightly as a guide for the beading needle. It is best to use thread close in colour to the background of the card.

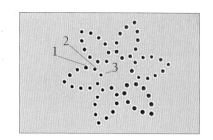

1. Lightly prick out the pattern using a pricking tool.

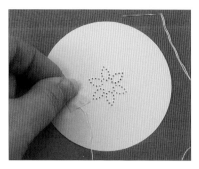

2. Tape the end of the thread to the back of the card.

3. Bring the thread through hole 2 and pick up a bead on your needle.

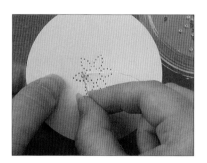

4. Secure the bead by going down hole 1.

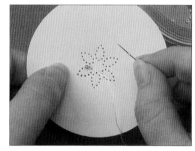

5. Bring the needle up in hole 3 and pick up another bead.

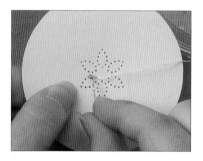

6. Go down in hole 2.

7. Move on to the next group of three holes and continue in the same way to finish the design. Secure the end of the thread at the back with tape as you did at the start.

Folding card

You may want to make your own cards. A cutting mat can be used to centre the fold of your card, or you can measure and mark the card. Whichever way you choose, accuracy is very important.

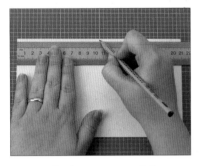

1. Mark the centre of the card with a pencil on the top and bottom edge, using the grid on your cutting mat as a guide.

2. Line up the ruler with the marks and score the card with a small embossing tool.

3. Fold along the scored line.

Making a border

1. To make a fine border, stick the design on to a larger piece of coloured paper using double-sided tape.

2. Use the grid on your cutting mat to measure the width of the border, and trim the paper using a ruler and craft knife.

3. Cut the other three sides to the same width, using the grid as a guide.

Tip
Take your time when trimming to ensure a neat cut.

Making gem flowers

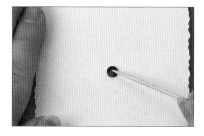  

1. Glue the gem for the flower centre on to paper, as shown on page 145.

2. Use a fine-tipped PVA glue applicator to place a circle of glue around the gem.

3. Use a cocktail stick to place oval pearls around the gem, pressing down towards the centre of the flower.

4. When the glue is dry, trim the paper away.

Dyeing lace

This technique allows you to colour pieces of lace the exact shade you need to match or complement your other embellishments. Here I use a pigment inkpad and a dauber.

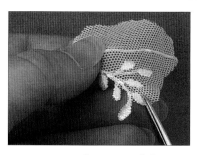  

1. Cut out the part of the lace using fine scissors.

2. Place it on kitchen paper to keep your work surface clean. Tap the dauber on to the pigment ink pad.

3. Transfer the colour to the lace by tapping with the dauber. Leave to dry.

The finished dyed lace.

149

Purple Parchment

This simple but effective card uses template PR0558 and incorporates deep purple parchment and gems to complement the pricked patterns.

You will need

Cream card blank, folded size
122 x 170mm (4¾ x 6¾in)

Ivory 160gsm (90lb) pastel
card, 120 x 150mm
(4¾ x 5⅞in)

Fancy-edged scissors,
cloud design

Pricking template PR0558

Masking tape

Pricking tool and mat

Deep purple parchment

Fine-tipped PVA glue
applicator and cocktail stick

Pencil, craft knife, metal ruler
and cutting mat

Crystal and purple teardrops

Crystal and purple 4mm
(⅛in) flat-backed faceted gems

Double-sided tape

1. Secure the template to the back of the ivory card, making sure the design is central. Prick the central design.

2. Cut down the sides of the card to 100mm (4in) wide using fancy-edged scissors. Make sure the sides match.

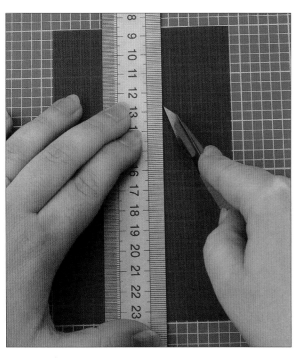

3. Measure, draw and cut out four pieces of purple parchment, 35 x 150mm ($1^3/_8$ x $5^7/_8$in) using a craft knife, metal ruler and cutting mat.

4. Use the pricking tool and mat to prick the daisy border from the template on two of the strips of parchment. The raised side will show.

5. Put double-sided tape on one edge of the front of a plain strip of purple parchment.

6. Stick the cream scalloped card on top so that the purple parchment just shows from underneath. Repeat the other side.

7. Using a fine-tipped PVA glue applicator, place dots of glue in the pricked petal shapes on the parchment. Place teardrop gems on the dots to form petals.

8. Stick circular gems on to form the flower centres. Repeat with the other pricked parchment strip.

9. When the glue is dry, turn the parchment over and place a dot of glue behind each gem.

Tip
Gluing parchment to the card by applying glue behind the gems prevents the glue from showing through the parchment.

10. Stick the parchment strips to the main artwork as shown. Mount the artwork centrally on the cream card blank using double-sided tape.

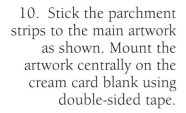

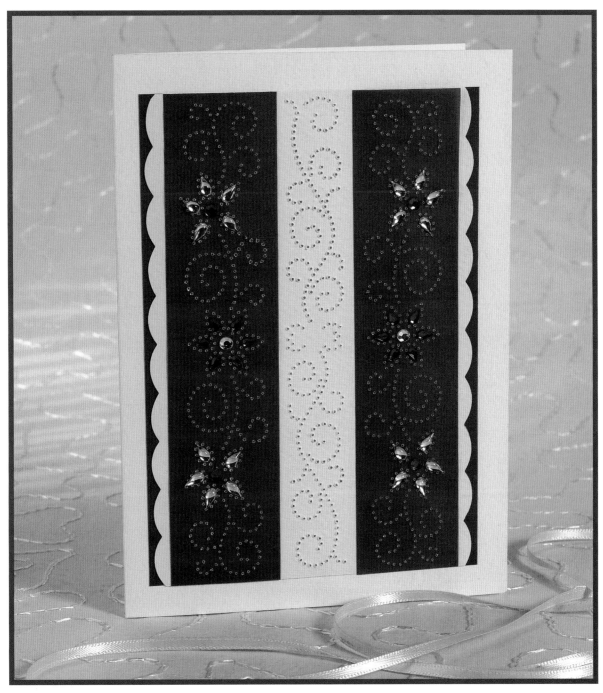

The finished card. The crystal gems are shown to their best advantage against the deep purple parchment. This is just one of many designs provided on template PR0558.

Top: This blue cameo card uses template PR0559 and a 120mm (4¾in) square card blank. I pricked out from the reverse side on two ivory 160gsm (90lb) pastel squares. I then mounted these on to pale blue parchment and decorated them with flat-backed faceted blue gems and pearls, surrounding the central blue cameo.

Bottom left: Here I cut out a gift tag blank using a template. I then pricked the blue panel in a lattice design with a decorative border, worked the lattice in thread, and glued on gem flowers.

Bottom right: For this bookmark, pink and ivory 160gsm (90lb) pastel paper was decorated in the same way as the main project card using PR0558 and mounted on purple parchment, which shows at the edges, with matching silk ribbons.

For this parchment fan, emboss around the top part of template PR0356 on to green parchment. Cut out the semi-circle and wind gold thread around the scallops from a hole made with a single hole punch as shown. Next, on cream parchment, emboss and cut out as before but then tape the template on to the front of the parchment and prick out the pattern, finishing with amber gems. Emboss the bottom part of the template on to another piece of cream parchment, cutting out, pricking and gluing amber teardrops as shown. Punch out a scallop-edged circle from green parchment, punch a central hole, cut it as shown and wind it with gold thread as for the larger semi-circle. Now assemble the four parts of the fan, finish with a gold tassel and place it on the cream card background embossed with window stencil LJ811.

Quilling

by Diane Crane

For as long as I can remember I have been fascinated by paper of all kinds. One of my earliest memories is of sitting on the floor at home surrounded by bits of paper and being completely absorbed as I worked away with scissors and glue for hours on end. Well, not much has changed, except that I now favour sitting at the dining room table!

Over twenty years ago, a friend introduced me to the craft of paper quilling. I was instantly drawn to this unusual way of working with paper. Shortly afterwards, I discovered the existence of the Quilling Guild, which fired my enthusiasm still further. Having tackled many of the quilling patterns available at the time, I began to take my first tentative steps in designing my own patterns, and as I experimented with different techniques, I realised that the possibilities were endless, limited only by the imagination of the quiller.

After a few years of quilling for my own pleasure, I was given the opportunity to share my discoveries with others through teaching a weekly class. Card making using quilled motifs has proved to be the most popular application of the craft. I frequently hear stories from quillers who have sent cards that were treasured, and sometimes even framed, by the recipients.

Quilling may not be the speediest of crafts, but it is certainly one of the most rewarding. Narrow strips of coloured paper are brought to life by the simple act of rolling, and a colourful world of paper coils and spirals opens up before your eyes. Everything you need is readily available: paper, scissors, glue and a willing set of fingers... so you can quill away to your heart's content!

Diane Crane

There are endless possibilities with paper. Here are a selection of cards illustrating the different effects you can achieve by using the quilling techniques demonstrated on the following pages.

Basic techniques

Before you begin, take a close look at a quilling strip. One side is smooth with edges that turn down slightly and the other side is not. Take some time to feel the difference between your fingers. Always roll with the smooth side on the outside, as this will help to make your quilling more uniform.

When you are rolling a strip for the first time, resist the temptation to roll too tightly. People think that if they relax the tension, the coil will unravel but this is not the case. The rolled paper will only expand to its natural size. Quilling is a bit like knitting in the sense that the patterns may be the same but everyone's tension is different! Practise with 3mm (¹⁄₈in) strips before attempting to quill with finer strips of paper.

You will need

Eight 3mm (¹⁄₈in) paper strips, 150mm (6in) long

One 2mm (³⁄₃₂in) paper strip, 150mm (6in) long

One 3mm (¹⁄₈in) paper strip, 450mm (17¾in) long

Quilling tool

Scissors

Fine-tip glue applicator

Cocktail sticks

Metric ruler

Tissue paper square, 50 x 50mm (2 x 2in)

Paper square, 20 x 20mm (¾ x ¾in)

Tile or jam jar lid

A basic coil

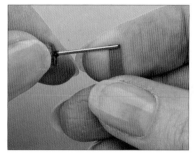

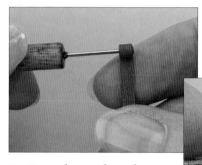

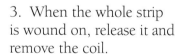

1. Line the strip up on the tool and start to turn.

2. Turn the tool so that the strip winds tightly around it.

3. When the whole strip is wound on, release it and remove the coil.

4. Put a dot of glue at the end of the strip. The less glue you use, the better your quilling will be!

5. Poke a cocktail stick into the coil and press against it as you close the coil.

A finished basic coil

Shapes

Each of the shapes that follow started off as a basic, glued coil. Hold the coil between your fingers and thumbs in the general shape before you make a definite pinch.

*Use your thumbs and forefingers to squeeze a coil into a **teardrop** shape.*

*Use both thumbs to make an **eye** shape.*

*Make another eye and then shape it into a **square**.*

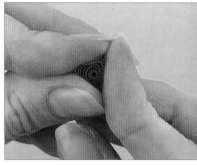

*Start with a teardrop and pinch it into a **triangle**.*

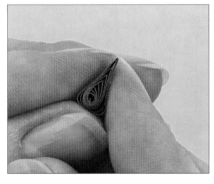

Make another teardrop and shape it into a ***long triangle***.

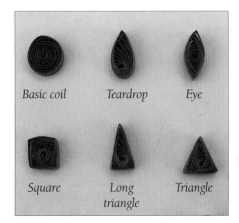

Basic coil	Teardrop	Eye
Square	Long triangle	Triangle

Tip

When making shapes, always pinch your coil at the glued join. This disguises the join and avoids it appearing in an awkward place.

Peg

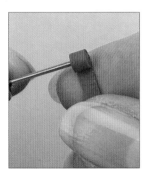

1. Roll a coil but do not let go when it is wound.

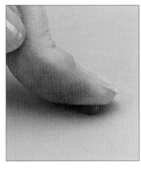

2. Glue the end of the strip down and then tap the peg down on the table.

3. Gently twist a cocktail stick in the hole to make the centre smooth.

A finished peg

Solid coil

1. Start off the coil by hand. Make it as tight as possible.

2. Now roll the coil by hand. Do not let go when it is wound.

3. Glue down the end. Your coil should be solid in the centre as shown.

A finished solid coil

Eccentric coil

1. Make a coil on the tool using an entire 450mm (17¾ in) strip, release it and glue down the end.

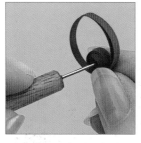

2. Now rewind the centre as shown and then let go.

3. Use a cocktail stick to gently even up the loops.

Tip
Making eccentric coils takes a little practice. Do not be discouraged if your first attempt is not as perfect as the one pictured. Keep trying!

4. Put a dab of glue on a tile or jam jar lid and place the coil on top.

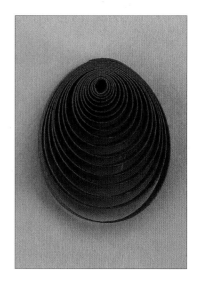

A finished eccentric coil

Spirals

1. Cut a 2mm ($^3/_{32}$in) strip down the centre to create two 1mm ($^1/_{32}$in) strips. Dampen the end of a 1mm ($^1/_{32}$in) strip with saliva and carefully wind it on to a piece of wire at a 45° angle.

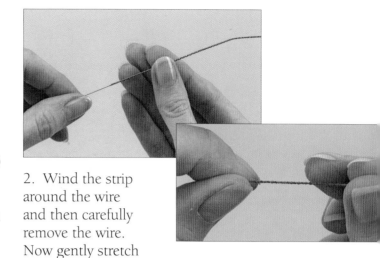

2. Wind the strip around the wire and then carefully remove the wire. Now gently stretch out the curled strip.

Spiral roses

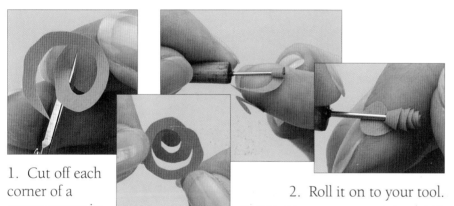

1. Cut off each corner of a paper square in a curve to make a circle. Then cut a spiral into the circle.

2. Roll it on to your tool.

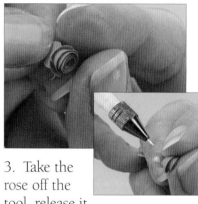

3. Take the rose off the tool, release it slightly and glue the end down.

Paper sticks

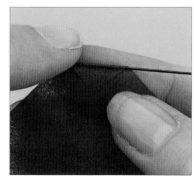

1. Fold the corner of a tissue paper square over a piece of wire and secure with glue.

2. Roll the tissue paper tightly around the wire.

3. Glue the end down and gently remove the wire.

Ready, Teddy, Go!

The shapes and swirls inside a coil intrigue me as much as the overall shape of the coil itself. In this project, I have used the eccentric coil method (see page 160) to make the body of the teddy. This technique is very useful when you are using a long strip of paper. If you left a large coil to its own devices, it would probably look rather untidy as the rolled layers of paper tend to gather at the edges of the coil, leaving an ugly space in the middle. By organising the layers into an eccentric coil, you can make it look much more attractive and it then becomes a design feature in itself.

Use the pattern above as a guide when you arrange your quilled shapes. The pattern is actual size.

Tip

When you are using more than one strip to make a large peg, make sure that you begin rolling from the same end of each strip as you separate it from the pack. This will prevent the finished peg from having a stripy appearance.

162

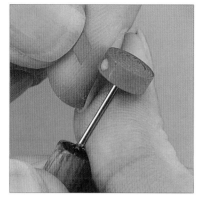

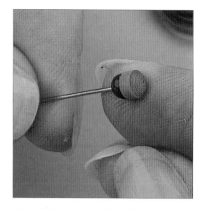

1. Start with the head. Roll a peg and glue it down. Glue on a fresh strip, roll it on and then secure with glue.

2. Roll two coils for the ears. Shape each coil into a crescent.

3. Make a solid coil for the snout and then push it on to a pin head to turn it into a dome. Now dab glue on the inside so that the snout keeps its shape. Allow to dry.

4. Make two coils for the legs. Shape each leg in two stages, as shown here.

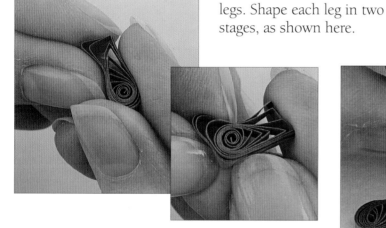

5. Make two more coils for the arms and shape them. Roll an eccentric coil for the body.

6. Mark the 99mm (3⁷⁄₈in) point on the shortest side of the blank card and fold the card in half. Chalk three yellow circles on your card (see page 165). Then glue pieces of the teddy in place one by one.

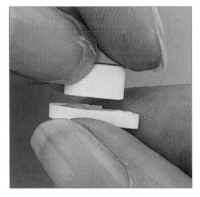

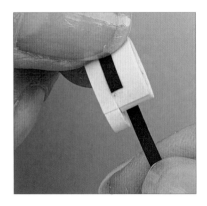

7. To make the crown of the hat, roll a 5mm ($^3/_{16}$in) cream strip into a coil and squeeze it flat.

8. Roll a looser coil from 2mm ($^3/_{32}$in) cream strip for the brim and flatten it. Glue the crown and brim together.

9. Wrap a 2mm ($^3/_{32}$in) black strip around the hat and glue it down. Trim off any excess black strip.

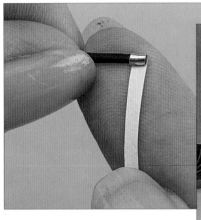

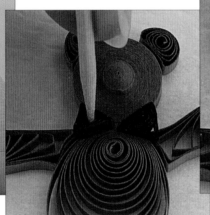

10. Make a paper stick (see page 161) from the tissue paper square and snip the ends straight. Then wrap a tiny piece of gold strip around one end and glue.

11. For the bow tie, make two triangles, dab glue on the back of each of them and position as shown using a cocktail stick.

12. Glue a small black square to the middle of the bow tie.

13. Glue on your bear's hat and cane. Then draw on his face with a fine black pen. Repeat steps 1 to 13 to make two more bears. Assemble them on the card and glue in place.

These energetic teddies look as though they have danced on to the card. By changing the position of the arms and legs you can create the illusion of movement. All of the bears have the same component parts as the one described in the steps, but you may need to alter the angle at the top of the arms and legs.

Teddies never seem to lose their popularity and card shops are happy hunting grounds for inspiration. Here, bears are busy catching butterflies, making daisy chains, and flying high above the clouds. The basic figure is the same on all the cards and I have used the chalk pastel technique to create all the backgrounds.

I have reduced the dimensions of the top and centre bears to make them look as though they are drifting up, up and away into the distance. To create the cloud effect, I used a piece of shaped card as a stencil.

Three-Dimensional Decoupage

by Dawn Allen

Cutting paper to create three-dimensional images started in the nineteenth century, when two identical images were placed on top of each other and separated by a mixture of paste and straw. In the mid- to late twentieth century this was developed into a three-dimensional art form by cutting pieces from several identical prints and layering the cut pieces on to a base image. The spaces between the layers were created using spots of silicone sealant.

Three-dimensional paper decoration has become very popular in recent years with the growing interest in hand-produced cards. Handmade cards are ideal for any occasion, and make a person feel extra special because you have taken the time and trouble to create a beautiful card just for them. In addition, you will have gained a great deal of pleasure from making it! A finished card can, of course, be framed as a permanent keepsake.

Three-dimensional greetings cards can be made from almost any paper image, such as prints, wrapping paper, or designs you have created yourself. You can use as few as four identical images to make a three-dimensional picture, and as many as twenty or thirty can be used to create a truly magnificent sculptured artwork. In general, the more images you use, the more detailed will be the finished picture.

Finally, coating the image with a paper glaze will produce an exquisite porcelain effect which not only enhances the colours but also protects your work.

The finished card can be decorated with one or more of the numerous embellishments that are now available, such as glitters, backing papers, buttons, eyelets, charms and ribbons. Craft stickers can be used to add a greeting or sentiment.

I wish you every success and enjoyment with your card making, and always remember that you will never make a mistake – it may be 'just a little bit different', that's all!

A selection of greetings cards that have been made using the techniques described in this book.

Basic techniques

There are several different methods of making three-dimensional cards. I am going to explain how to use pre-printed sheets, step-by-step sheets, outline craft stickers and rubber stamps. All the materials used in these projects can be obtained through good craft outlets.

Before starting on the projects it is a good idea to practise the basic techniques used in cutting, shaping and mounting.

Cutting using a craft knife

There are two methods of cutting: using either a pair of sharp-pointed scissors or a craft knife. It can be difficult to cut fine, intricate shapes with scissors, whereas if you learn to cut correctly with a craft knife you can achieve much greater precision, and the finished product looks far better. You will need a knife that is capable of taking a standard size 10A blade, which is flexible and which has a very sharp cutting point.

The basic technique for cutting using a craft knife is very simple. If you pick up a pencil and start to write or draw, you will notice that you are holding the pencil at a slight angle –hold your knife in exactly the same way.

You will need a board to cut on. Do not use a chopping board, bread board or anything with a hard surface as this will only blunt the blade and leave raised edges under your work which will make cutting difficult. The best surface is a self-healing cutting mat which, as the name implies, seals itself after a fine cut and therefore retains a smooth, flat surface.

You will need
Cutting mat
Craft knife that holds a size 10A blade

Tip
Always use a sharp blade in your craft knife – a blunt one may tear the paper. You will achieve far better results if you always start a project with a new blade.

1. When you begin cutting, relax, hold the knife comfortably at an angle of about 30° to the cutting surface and cut gently in a flowing movement around the outline of the shape. In this way you are effectively bevelling the paper by cutting away the underneath part so that the white edge of the paper will not be visible.

2. Start at the top and work down the right-hand side of the piece to be cut. Turn the paper as you cut, following the outline.

3. Keep the knife on the right-hand side of the cut so the cutting line is always visible. There is no need to press too hard.

Tip
Reverse Step 3 if you are left-handed.

Furring and feathering

You can use either a craft knife or scissors to create the effect of fur or feathers, though a knife will always give you a finer finish – you do not want your animal to end up looking as though it needs grooming!

To achieve this effect successfully, the angle of your knife or scissors is important.

1. Angle the knife from side to side, making a criss-cross pattern.

2. Lengthen and shorten the cuts as necessary to obtain a fur-like effect.

Tip
With this technique it is sometimes necessary to colour in the edge. Do this using watercolour pens/pencils. Always use a shade lighter than the actual image, and colour from the back to hide any white edges.

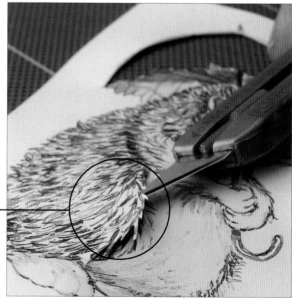

3. The closer you make the cuts, the finer the furring/feathering will be.

Shaping

Shaping is an essential part of three-dimensional picture sculpture. To achieve natural-looking shapes you need to visualise the subject in real life and then re-create it in three dimensions. Use wooden shaping tools in conjunction with a small foam pad or an eraser to avoid creasing or tearing the piece you are shaping.

Only the top pieces of the image (the pieces that are not covered by another piece) need to be shaped. To achieve the required shape, place the cut piece face down on either an eraser or a foam pad and gently roll it into the required shape using the shaped end of a shaping tool.

Be gentle and keep the shaping slight; if you over-shape the piece it will not fit completely over the piece behind it. When you have achieved the desired result, hold the piece in position with tweezers to see if the shape is correct. If it is, then apply; if not then re-shape it and try again.

You will need
Wooden shaping tools
Pencil eraser
Foam pad

For a firm, rounded shape such as leaves or berries, apply hard shaping using a pencil eraser and a pointed shaping tool.

For softer curves, apply soft shaping using a foam pad and a rounded shaping tool.

Mounting

There are two methods of mounting the pieces: using either 3D foam squares or silicone sealant.

Sealant will give a better result, as you can control the height and width of the sealant by applying it to your work using a cocktail stick. Use approximately 3–5mm (¼in) of silicone between the base print and the first layer, and approximately 2–3mm (⅛in) between subsequent layers. If you can, leave the first layer to dry for five to ten minutes. By leaving this piece to cure it makes it easier to apply the rest of the pieces.

You will need
Silicone sealant
3mm (⅛in) 3D foam squares
Cocktail sticks for applying the silicone sealant
Angled and straight tweezers
Craft knife

If you are using 3D foam squares, apply a square to the back of the piece, and gently lift off the backing using the tip of a craft knife.

Tip
If you are using 3D foam squares, put two squares together to obtain extra height.

Once you have applied either silicone sealant or foam squares to your cut-out piece, use tweezers to place the piece on your image and if necessary use a clean cocktail stick for fine adjustments. If you have used silicone sealant, do not use your fingers to push the piece down on to the work as it will flatten and spread the glue over the edges; use a cocktail stick.

If you are using silicone sealant, transfer the required amount of sealant on to a cocktail stick.

Apply it to your work using a rolling motion.

Tip
Keep the silicone away from the edges of the print to avoid it being seen on the finished card.

Glazing

Glazing can certainly enhance a card by creating a porcelain effect, but it is really a matter of personal preference. It is not always necessary to glaze the whole card; select the parts that you feel would be accentuated by glazing. Remember always to test a scrap piece of your work first to make sure it is colourfast.

It is necessary to apply only a single coat of glaze. Allow three to four hours for the glaze to dry, and remember to clean your brush immediately after use using a spirit-based brush cleaner.

You will need

High-gloss paper glaze
Camel hair paintbrush
Spirit-based brush cleaner

1. Load the paintbrush with glaze, transfer it to the image and allow the glaze to drop on to the image from a height of about 0.5cm (¼in).

2. Pull the glaze down the image with the brush. Repeat until the glazing is complete.

Caution
To use high-gloss paper glaze safely, use it only in a well-ventilated area, avoid breathing in the fumes directly, and keep the glaze well away from naked flames. Children must not be allowed to use paper glaze unsupervised.

The finished glazed flower.

Purple Pansies

Using identical images rather than step-by-step sheets to create a three-dimensional card gives you the chance to be really creative! You can put in as much or as little detail as you wish simply by varying the number of pieces you cut out – the more pieces you use, the more detailed your design will be. You can also, of course, use as many copies of the image as you need.

Begin by visualising the finished card, and decide which parts of the image you want to stand out from the background. Look at the details – layering the tiny dewdrop on this bunch of pansies really made it stand out and enhanced the beauty of the whole card. The next step is to plan how you will cut out your pieces. Always start with the layers at the back of the picture and work your way forwards.

All this takes time, but it is well worth the effort when you see the end result and know that it is all your own work!

You will need

Pre-printed sheet
(Pansies III by Reina)

Dark purple A6 card blank,
105 x 148mm (4¼ x 6in)

Light purple card,
80 x 120mm (3¼ x 4¾in)

Cream card, 90 x 130mm
(3½ x 5in)

Small gold circle craft stickers

Permanent adhesive dots or
double-sided tape

Silicone sealant

Tweezers, straight and angled

Cocktail sticks

Craft knife and spare blades

Cutting mat

Fancy-edged scissors

Shaping tools

Eraser

Foam pad

1. Cut out one complete image from the sheet using the cutting technique described on pages 170–171. Cut approximately 2mm (⅛in) out from the edge of the image to create a light border when the image is attached to the card. This will form your base print.

2. Cut out a second complete image, this time cutting close to the edge.

3. Decide which parts of your picture you want to stand out, and cut these out from the remaining two images on the sheet. Begin with the parts that are at the back of the picture, and gradually move forwards to those that are at the front.

4. Cut pieces from the base print if you need to, as this will be covered up by the top layers of the image.

The complete set of cut-out shapes ready for making into the three-dimensional image.

5. Softly shape the edges of the leaves on the second complete image you cut out using the barrel of a shaping tool.

6. Make sure you have not made the image too small through over-shaping by holding it over the base print. (You can make the image flatter by gently flicking back the sides.)

7. Apply three spots of silicone sealant to the back of the image and attach it to the base.

8. Starting with the back flower, gently shape each petal by rolling the shaping tool over the base (but not the outer part) of the petal.

9. Place a spot of silicone sealant in the centre of the petal.

177

10. Attach the petal to the base flower. Tilt it gently towards the centre of the flower, raising up the outer edge, to give a three-dimensional effect. Apply the remaining petals to the back flower in the same way. Allow the silicone sealant to dry.

11. Shape the leaf gently using the eraser and the pointed shaping tool. Roll it on the diagonal to give a pleasing shape to the leaf.

12. Attach the leaf to the base using a single spot of silicone sealant.

13. Shape the dewdrop on the eraser using the pointed shaping tool. Use circular movements to give the dewdrop a smooth, rounded shape.

14. Apply a tiny spot of silicone sealant to the back of the dewdrop and, using the angled tweezers, carefully lay it in position on the base print.

15. Build up the remaining parts of the image in the same way.

16. Prepare the card, attaching the mounts using either permanent adhesive dots or double-sided tape, and attach the three-dimensional image using silicone sealant. Finish by adding a small gold circle to each corner of the purple mount.

Purple Pansies

The cream-coloured border around the pansies was very easy to achieve and gives this card a much lighter feel. It is accentuated by the cream border around the purple mat mount, and the addition of details like the raised dewdrop and the tiny gold circles at each corner of the background.

©2005, Reina, N.Y.

Flowers have always been a popular subject for greetings cards. All of these were made from pre-printed sheets, and they show how various types of card blanks and embellishments can be used to enhance, but not detract from, the intrinsic beauty of the three-dimensional image.

Top row and bottom right ©2005 Reina, N.Y.; bottom left ©2005 Morehead, Inc.

Iris Folding

by Michelle Powell

The first time I saw an iris folded card, I was mesmerised by the swirling, spiralling layers of paper. The rich, intricate design looked very complicated, with layers of interest in every fold of the beautiful handmade paper. When I set about trying to make the folded panel, I was amazed at how simple it was to create such a complex-looking design, just by following a basic pattern.

The overlapping, spiralling layers of folded paper that create an iris folded design look similar to the iris aperture in a camera lens, which is how iris folding got its name.

Like many paper crafts, iris folding originated in the Netherlands. The inside of Dutch envelopes are often printed with a pretty pattern, and strips of this paper were used to create iris folded designs.

My attraction to iris folding comes from the fact that it utilises all those wonderful types and colours of paper now available. The simple folded design enhances the beauty of the papers used, letting them speak for themselves rather than consigning them to a border or a background. I am a self-confessed paper junky: I like nothing more than browsing through books of printed paper or touching sheets of vellum, pearlescent paper or glittery card. You do not need to spend a fortune, though; iris folding can be done with wrapping paper or whatever type of paper appeals to you, as long as it is not too thick.

The project in this section will guide you through the basic technique of iris folding, explaining how to cut, fold, and most importantly, position all those wonderful papers. When you have mastered the basic technique, let your imagination run wild and try creating designs in hand-cut shaped apertures, combine techniques for more effects or produce three-dimensional shaped cards with dazzling iris panels. Most of all, have fun iris folding!

Basic techniques

Some basic crafting skills will help with the project in this book. There are many ways to complete these basic techniques, but I have shown you the way I find easiest.

Folding and scoring card

1. Use a ruler and pencil to measure and mark your card to the size and shape that you need.

2. Place your work on a cutting mat and use a craft knife and ruler to cut out the card.

3. Mark the centre point at the top and bottom of the card using a pencil.

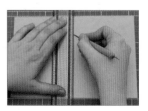

4. Place a ruler on your card to join these marks and use an embossing stylus to score the card.

5. Fold the card, making sure that the top edges line up. You can trim the card slightly if the edges are a little out of line. Use your thumbnail to reinforce the fold.

Transferring patterns

To transfer patterns, I prefer to create a set of card templates. It takes a little longer, but your templates can be used many times over.

1. Trace the pattern directly from the book using tracing paper and a pencil.

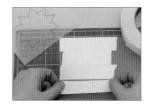

2. Cover a piece of thin card with double-sided tape and stick the tracing paper pattern to it.

3. Cut round the pattern using scissors or a craft knife and cutting mat.

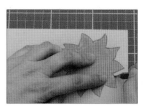

4. Draw around the template on to the correct coloured paper or card.

Cutting and folding paper strips

Cut strips of paper are used for most of the projects in this book, they are quick and simple to make. When using very translucent vellum, cut the strips, but do not fold.

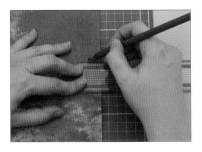

1. Use a ruler and pencil to measure strips 1.5cm (⁵⁄₈in) wide (some projects will require wider strips).

2. Use a craft knife, cutting mat and ruler to cut the strips. It does not matter if they are a bit wobbly as you use the folded rather than the cut edge.

3. Fold approximately one third of the paper over. Most papers can be folded by hand, but for stiff papers, place a ruler on the strip, score along it using an embossing stylus, then fold.

Making a key

A key is useful to help you remember which coloured strip goes where when you are making up the iris folded panel.

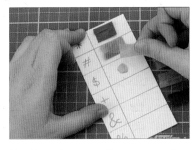

1. Mark up a piece of card with six rows and two columns. The size does not matter, as this is for your reference only.

2. Draw each of the symbols used in this section in the left column. They are *, #, $, +, &, %. If you plan to do a lot of iris folding it may be worth laminating this key.

3. Attach a small square of each of your chosen coloured paper strips next to the correct symbol using adhesive putty. If your iris panel has four colours, use the top four; if it has five or six, use the top five or all six rows. After completing your iris design, remove the strips so that you can use the key again.

Oriental Flowers

Iris folding is not limited to a square shape; rectangle, triangle, oval and circle apertures all add interest to the iris design. If you want to create a personalised card, iris folding creates a perfect background; the addition of a motif such as a vase of flowers, wedding cake, boat, fish or pram can adapt your card for specific occasions.

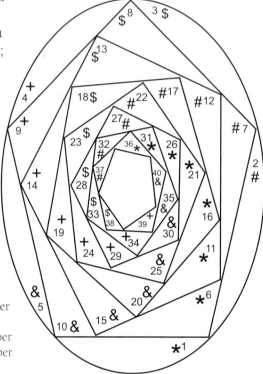

Folding template shown full size
KEY:
* Sage handmade paper
# Cream swirl paper
$ Green patterned paper
+ Beige handmade paper
& Green dot paper

You will need

Cream card 21 x 15cm (8¼ x 6in)

Green card 12 x 12cm (4¾ x 34¾in)

Cream pearlescent card

Patterned papers: sage and beige handmade, cream swirl, green and green dot

Cream pearlescent vellum

White pearlescent paper

Brown mottled paper

Packing card

3 green flat-backed gemstones

Small and medium flower punches and leaf punch

Craft knife and cutting mat

Ruler, pencil and scissors

Glue stick or glue roller

Double-sided tape

3D foam tape

Adhesive putty

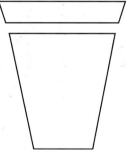

Motif patterns

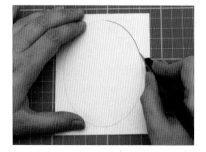

1. Cut a rectangle of cream pearlescent card 11.5 x 8.5cm (4½ x 3³⁄₈in). Trace the outer edge of the oval folding template and transfer on to the cream card. Cut the oval aperture using a craft knife and cutting mat.

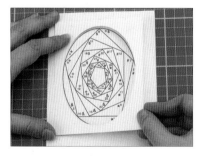

2. Place your aperture face down onto the folding template and attach it with adhesive putty.

3. Cut and fold five coloured strips as shown on page 185. For this project you will need approximately a 35cm (13¾in) length for each of the five colours, but this does not have to be one long length.

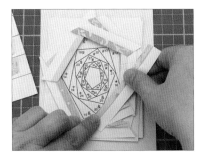

4. Make a paper key (see page 185). Create the iris folding design. Remember to use each of the five colours in turn before starting on the next loop.

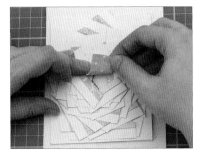

5. Continue, following the numerical sequence and creating one full loop each time until you reach the middle. Cut a small piece of paper and glue it over the central hole. Remove from the template.

6. Cover the back of the iris folding with double-sided tape; this will help to hold all the pieces in position.

7. Cut a rectangle of green card 12 x 9cm (4¾ x 3½in). Remove the backing from the tape and stick the iris folded piece centrally on the green card.

8. Use an A6 folded cream card blank or cut and fold your own. Cut a strip of green patterned paper 4.5 x 15cm (1¾ x 6in). Attach this using double-sided tape on the left-hand side of the cream card.

9. Cut a piece of cream pearl vellum 5 x 15cm (2 x 6in) and tear down one of the long sides.

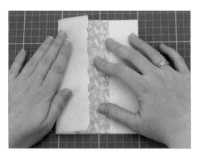

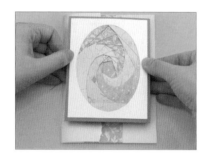

10. Place narrow double-sided tape on the back of the cream card near the fold. Attach the cut edge of the vellum to this tape. Fold the vellum over to the front of the card.

11. Use 3D foam tape to attach the iris folding and mount to the front of the card. This will also hold the torn vellum flap in place.

12. Punch six medium flowers from white pearlescent paper, and three small flowers from cream pearlescent vellum. Punch four leaves from green card.

13. To assemble the flowers, use tiny pieces of double-sided tape to stick two medium flower shapes on top of each other. Add a small cream flower in the centre and a flat-backed gemstone on top.

14. Fold each leaf in half and open out, then attach it to the back of the flower using double-sided tape.

15. Place a strip of wide double-sided tape, 10cm (4in) long on the edge of a piece of packing card. Peel off the backing and stick brown mottled paper to the tape.

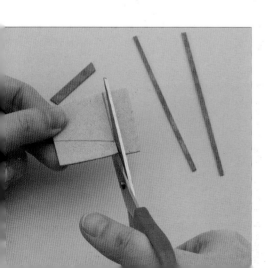

16. Create templates of the plant pot and rim and draw round them on to the covered packing card. Cut out the pot and rim. Also cut a 2mm (1/8in) strip of the covered card approximately 10cm (4in) long for the sticks.

Tip

Add double-sided tape to the back of your card before cutting out small motifs or strips. This is much easier than trying to cut small pieces of tape to fit afterwards.

17. Assemble the pot and sticks using double-sided tape, add the flowers and attach the motif to the front of your card using 3D foam tape.

This card uses five patterned papers to create an oval iris folded background for a simple pot of flowers.

These folding templates for the cards opposite are shown full size.

Add a specific motif such as a wedding cake or pram to make your iris folded cards appropriate for different occasions.

Index